Health and Safety in Early Years and Childcare

Contextualising health and safety legislation within the Early Years Foundation Stage

Bernadina Laverty and Catherine Reay

NCB's vision is a society in which all children and young people are valued and their rights are respected. By advancing the well-being of all children and young people across every aspect of their lives, NCB aims to:

- reduce inequalities in childhood
- ensure children and young people have a strong voice in all matters that affect their lives
- promote positive images of children and young people
- enhance the health and well-being of all children and young people
- encourage positive and supportive family, and other environments.

NCB has adopted and works within the UN Convention on the Rights of the Child.

Published by the National Children's Bureau

National Children's Bureau, 8 Wakley Street, London EC1V 7QE
Tel: 0207 843 6000
Website: www.ncb.org.uk
Registered charity number: 258825

NCB works in partnership with Children in Scotland (www.childreninscotland.org.uk) and Children in Wales (www.childreninwales.org.uk).

© National Children's Bureau 2014

ISBN: 978 1 909391 00 0

British Library Cataloguing in Publication Data
A catalogue record for this book is available from the British Library

Typeset by Saxon Graphics Ltd, Derby, UK

Disclaimer

This book is intended solely as an informational resource for early years and childcare staff. The information contained within this book has been researched and compiled from reliable sources. It is believed to be current at the time of writing. The book is intended to inform rather than advise. It provides signposts and links to useful resources. It does not negate fulfilment of statutory duties by the employer, self-employed people, employees and people in control of premises. The enclosed information may be used to assist in making informed decisions, but the user should make independent judgements appropriate to any given setting. The authors take no responsibility for the consequence of any error, any loss or damage suffered by the users of any information published in this book. The authors take no responsibility for inspection gradings or enforcement outcomes in settings.

All links and website details last accessed 26 February 2014 unless otherwise stated.

Contents

Dedication

For Phil, in memoriam, 2 July 2012

About the authors

Bernadina Laverty is an early years/childcare consultant and freelance inspector. She has 18 years of inspection experience, covering the full range of early years provisions. She has a variety of childcare experience having worked in nurseries, schools, a residential unit and with a local authority early years service. She has devised and delivered training, both in-house and as a National Vocational Qualification tutor and assessor. She holds a BA (Hons) degree in Early Childhood Studies. She has particular interests in improving quality and health and safety in the early years.

Catherine Reay is an environmental health professional working as a freelance consultant. She has 25 years' experience in health and safety and food safety disciplines. She has worked in both the public and private sectors. Catherine has extensive experience in auditing health and safety systems and in accident investigation. She has devised and delivered bespoke health and safety training and health and safety systems across business sectors including the service and manufacturing industries. She is a member of, and a registered tutor with, the Chartered Institute of Environmental Health Officers. She has a Diploma in Environmental Health and Management Studies. She is committed to providing practical health and safety guidance to this sector.

Acknowledgements

In combining both the Early Years Foundation Stage (EYFS) and health and safety legislation, we hope this book helps to clarify and put into perspective what is required to make sure children can play safely and achieve their full potential in your settings. We may both come from different inspection backgrounds, but we share a common belief that children's safety and welfare is paramount. Working collaboratively from two different safety perspectives has been challenging, inspirational and provides a unique opportunity to explore and discover much common ground.

We recognise and admire that many providers are striving for quality and trying to adhere to all requirements, sometimes without consistency or clarity of information. We hope that this book goes some way in supporting providers to deliver, safe, stimulating and challenging learning experiences for the benefit of all children and their families. Thank you for the inspiration and motivation for us to write together.

In particular we would both like to thank:

- Paula McMahon and Daniel Kelly at NCB for their patience, understanding and for gently guiding two novice authors through the writing and publication process

- our friends and families, who have supported, encouraged and motivated us during testing times

- Pete, Al, Sinead and Catherine for tolerating the lack of domesticity during the writing process and encouraging us along the way

- Fionnuala, whose motivation and wisdom helped us to finish the book

- our critical reader, who never complained about proofreading chapters and whose feedback was invaluable; we are indebted. You know who you are

- Jenny, TK, Linda, Jon, Emma, Craig, Richard, Nathan, Roy, Jackie and Tony – it was a privilege to work with you all

- the providers we have visited over the course of our careers. Thank you for the professional insight, opportunities to observe your practice, debates and discussions. We are privileged.

Introduction

Who is the book for?

This book is intended for all staff working within the Early Years Foundation Stage (EYFS) or environmental health area. It will be useful for senior staff and managers for auditing, improving standards and preparing for inspection. It is also helpful to other staff including childminders as it clearly outlines responsibilities within the legislative framework. Registration and enforcement officers/inspectors will also find it valuable as a reference tool.

What is the book about?

This is an innovative book bringing two inspection perspectives together. It contextualises and cements health and safety legislation with the EYFS. The book takes the reader through key safety points, why they are required, how to comply with the requirement and a means of assessing compliance and taking corrective action.

The main themes are as follows.

- Taking ownership – personal responsibility for safeguarding children and meeting the welfare requirements and legal duties.
- Enforcement – the consequences of not ensuring children's safety and well-being.
- Applying the principles – a common sense approach; navigating through the legislation with examples and audit tools.
- Evaluation and reflection – self-audit and nurturing an ongoing safety conscious culture.

How the book can be used

This is a practical book that can be referred to by individual chapters as needs arise or as an aid to inspection. There are pointers under headings to legislation prompts.

The Childcare Act 2006 and associated regulations set out the requirements with which providers must comply and against which their provision is regulated. This includes the Statutory Framework for the EYFS. Providers may be registered on the Early Years Register (EYR) and/or the Childcare Register which has two parts: the compulsory part (CCR) and the voluntary part (VCR).

The EYFS prompts are below.

 EYFS

Childcare Register Requirements childcare providers on non-domestic or domestic premises; and childminders and home childcarers (abbreviated as CR).

 CR

The health and safety and food safety the legislation prompts are below.

➡ Health & Safety at Work etc. Act 1974 Section 2(1) and relevant regulations.

Each chapter includes ongoing prompts to help the reader clarify, evaluate and reflect.

Audit tools accompany each chapter of this book to assist with evaluation, reflection and action planning. These can be found in the Resources section of the NCB Publications web page, at the below link.

www.ncb.org.uk/what-we-do/publications/support-resources/health-and-safety-in-early-years-and-childcare

1 Management responsibilities

'Please keep me safe. This simple but profoundly important hope is the very minimum upon which every child and young person should be able to depend' (The Lord Laming. 'The Protection of Children in England: A Progress Report'. 12 March 2009).

Children's vulnerability means adults must be proactive in taking action to ensure children are protected from abuse and neglect. The EYFS safeguarding and welfare requirements encompass other legislation that must be adhered to. This chapter highlights the importance of safeguarding children and the responsibilities of the registered person (employer) and management team.

The Health and Safety at Work etc. Act 1974 contains defined responsibilities that employers must meet. Although these responsibilities are common sense, employers may be unaware of their duties and may inadvertently fail to meet them. The duties placed on employers under the main act are echoed in specific regulations. This chapter gives an overview of all aspects of management responsibilities.

Child protection

 EYFS 3.1–3.4 and CR 1.1 CR 2.1, CR 2.3

This section encapsulates the need for high quality practice in all settings. Necessary steps to keep children safe and well are to:

- safeguard children
- ensure adult suitability
- promote good health
- manage behaviour
- maintain records, policies and procedures.

All policies and procedures must be in writing (except for childminders only registered on the Early Years Register (EYR). Schools are not required to have separate EYFS procedures providing requirements are already covered. Written policies and procedures must be up to date and personalised to your setting. Make sure induction procedures for all new staff, students, apprentices and volunteers includes their safeguarding duties. Up-to-date contact numbers for local statutory children's services agencies that all staff can access must be included.

 Remember

Have you considered how all families can access this information including those who have English as an additional language?

Policies and procedures

 EYFS 3.4 and CR 2.1

Staff need to be aware of issues and challenges within children's home lives in order to be able to instigate support swiftly. Therefore, forging effective relationships with parents and carers is crucial. Staff have a duty to respect and promote children's rights, individuality and uniqueness in all circumstances.

Remember

The serious case review into Daniel Pelka's death highlights numerous missed opportunities to intervene and protect Daniel: 'In this case, professionals needed to "think the unthinkable" and to believe and act upon what they saw in front of them, rather than accept parental versions of what was happening at home without robust challenge' (Lock, R. 2013, p6. Coventry Safeguarding Children Board. September 2013).

Robust procedures must be followed and be written in accordance with the relevant Local Safeguarding Children Board (LSCB) and made available to all adults in your setting and parents and carers. This policy must reflect procedures to be followed in the event of an allegation being made against a member of staff.

An explicit statement about the use of cameras and mobile phones within the setting must also be included. Have clear, common-sense guidance about when cameras and mobile phones can be used. For example, outings, emergencies, special events etc. Include a list of examples in the staff induction pack.

Remember

Safeguarding must be a priority. Inspectors may look at your child protection policy and may question leadership and management if any of the documentation does not belong to your setting.

Designated lead for safeguarding

 EYFS 3.5

A lead practitioner must be nominated to take responsibility for safeguarding. This lead role involves liaison with statutory bodies and offering support and advice to staff within your establishment. A recognised safeguarding training course that includes recognising the signs of abuse and neglect must be completed by the lead practitioner.

Remember

The appointed lead person needs to be experienced and confident in providing support, advice and guidance to all staff on an ongoing basis. Ensure you can justify your decision making when appointing lead people.

Training

 EYFS 3.6

All staff must receive training and guidance on safeguarding policies and procedures. This must include advice on recognising signs and symptoms of abuse and neglect and how to take concerns forward.

Remember

The serious case review into Keanu Williams' death highlights that 'Keanu was seen by staff in the nursery early in the New Year 2011 with a number of marks and bruises on his body and was described as "distressed". No referral was made and clear guidelines and procedures were not followed as staff believed the explanations put forward by Rebecca Shuttleworth and did not take action to protect Keanu. Keanu died four days later of multiple injuries sustained over a period of time' (Lundberg, B. 2013, p8. Serious case review Birmingham; Keanu Williams. http://www.lscbbirmingham.org.uk/images/stories/downloads/executive-summaries/Case_25__Final_Overview_Report_02.10.13.pdf.)

Signs of abuse and neglect could be:

- changes in children's behaviour
- unexplained marks and bruising
- deterioration in children's well-being
- concerns about a child's home life
- children's comments/conversations that worry you.

Staff code of conduct alerts could be:

- staff behaviour that is inappropriate, including sexually lewd comments, unhealthy interest in particular children
- inappropriate attention/interaction with children, sharing indecent/inappropriate texts, images.

Put 'safeguarding' on the agenda for team, supervision and appraisal meetings. Ensure you keep evidence/notes about such meetings and support staff in being open and honest about their concerns.

Remember

A 'whistle blowing' policy is important to enable staff to escalate concerns about staff attitudes or practice further. This takes courage, but all staff need to be clear that 'a child's welfare is paramount' (Children Act 1989). See http://www.ofsted.gov.uk/contact-us/whistleblower-hotline.

Statutory guidance

 EYFS 3.7

The government has produced statutory guidance 'Working together to safeguard children' (DCSF 2010) to encourage collaborative working between all professionals, children's families and to escalate concerns quickly. It is crucial that all settings, including childminders, adopt their own policies and procedures that clearly outline expectations of what will happen in the event of a safeguarding concern. Your staff must be familiar with these policies – an inspector may ask any member of staff. Think about devising protocols for working with other professionals and access to support services.

 Remember

Notify your local authority designated officer (LADO) with any relevant information about people who pose a risk to vulnerable groups in order to identify and bar unsuitable adults from working with children. Contact the Disclosure and Barring Service (DBS) for further advice. For more information see 'Working Together to Safeguard Children. A guide to inter-agency working to safeguard and promote the welfare of children (March 2013). http://www.education.gov.uk/aboutdfe/statutory/ g00213160/working-together-to-safeguard-children.

Informing Ofsted of allegations

 EYFS 3.8 and CR 13

Ofsted must be informed of all allegations of serious harm or abuse. This could be by any person who is looking after children or has contact with children in a registered setting. The allegations must be reported regardless of whether they relate to onsite or elsewhere. Remember it is the person who is the threat to a child.

 Law

If you fail to notify Ofsted within 14 days of allegations of serious harm or abuse you have committed an offence and could be prosecuted.

Childminders

The above guidance applies to childminders who also need to consider:

 EYFS 3.3

This section in the EYFS states there is no requirement for childminders to have a written policies and procedures. However, they must be able to explain and demonstrate their policies and procedures to parents, carers and others, such as Ofsted inspectors. They must also ensure any assistants understand and follow procedures.

 CR 2.1

However, if a childminder is registered on the Childcare register, under CR 2.1, it outlines that 'childminders must keep and implement a written statement of procedures to be followed for the protection of children, intended to safeguard the children being cared for from abuse or neglect'. Therefore, if you are registered on the childcare register, robust, written child protection procedures are needed.

EYFS 3.5

Childminders are deemed to be the lead person for safeguarding children.

Staff ratios

 EYFS 3.27–EYFS 3.38, CR 4.3 and CR 4.4

Children must be appropriately supervised at all times and staff must ensure all children's individual needs are met. Parents and carers need to be aware about arrangements for children's supervision and be told about staff changes.

 Remember

Staff must be able to see and/or hear children in order to supervise them. For example, children playing inside a den or play house may not be visible, but staff must be able to hear them and help immediately if they need to.

 Law

Health and safety legislation applies here for staff aged under 18.

 EYFS 3.28

Staffing ratios can only include staff aged 17 or over. Students on long-term placements, apprentices or volunteers may be included in ratios provided they have demonstrated competence. You may be required to produce evidence, such as supervision notes, to support your assessment of competence.

 EYFS 3.29 and CR 1.7, CR 1.10 and CR 1.12

Only staff working directly with children can be counted in ratios and qualification requirements. CR 1.7 outlines that at least two suitable persons who have attained the age of 18 are present on the premises at all times.

 Remember

From September 2012, in most cases, Ofsted no longer sets out the numbers and ages of children that registered providers may care for through conditions of registration. Registered providers decide how many children they can care for in line with the legal requirements. Ofsted will check you continue to meet the requirements at inspection. For full details on the numbers and ages of children that providers on the Early Years and Childcare Registers may care for, including exceptions, see http://www.ofsted.gov.uk/resources/factsheet-childcare-numbers-and-ages-of-children-providers-early-years-and-childcare-registers-may-care-for.

Ratios need to be met at all times of the day. Sometimes the beginning and end of day, can be difficult to plan for. For example, if staff are late, or need to leave early. You must ensure you have contingency plans in place.

 Remember

Administration staff based in an office, a cook working in a kitchen or an off-site committee member cannot be counted as part of the daily ratios.

 EYFS 3.30–EYFS 3.38

The EYFS outlines specific guidance on qualifications levels dependent upon age of children and hours of operation. Qualifications need to be classed as full and relevant – working towards a qualification does not meet the requirement for ratios.

Childminders

The above guidance applies to childminders, who also need to consider:

 EYFS 3.39–EYFS 3.41

Childminders may care for a maximum of six children under the age of eight at any one time. Within this number you can care for three 'young' children, with only one of whom can be a baby under 12 months (a young child is classed as young until 1 September following their fifth birthday).

 CR 1.10 and CR 1.11

Childminders and home childcarers must be aged 18 or over and childminders must ensure that anyone aged under 18 caring for children is supervised at all times by a person who has reached the age of 18.

 EYFS 3.40

Exceptions may be made to ratios if the childminder needs to care for young siblings, such as twins. Childminders need to demonstrate to parents and carers and, inspectors, that every child's individual needs can still be met. Children under five who attend full-time school and attend the setting for after school and holiday care would not be classed as a 'young' child.

 EYFS 3.41

If a childminder employs an assistant, they must have written permission from parents and carers for the assistant to have any sole charge of their children. Assistants may only have sole charge of children for no more than two hours in total, in a single day. For more information see 'Factsheet: childcare – Childcare on domestic premises'. http://www.ofsted.gov.uk/resources/factsheet-childcare-childcare-domestic-premises

 Law

You must not assume that you can care for all children from the same family if this would breach ratios. You must inform Ofsted of your intentions and allow an assessment to be made. Twins count as two children, therefore caring for twin babies without prior approval could mean that you are committing an offence. This could also make your public liability insurance invalid.

Key person

 EYFS 1.11 and EYFS 3.26

Each individual child must be assigned a key person who understands their role and responsibilities to meet children's individual needs. Each

child's specific temperament, interests, routines and preferred way of learning must be respected and planned for by the key person. The key person needs to build trusting relationships with children's families to:

- exchange information
- meet children's individual needs
- instigate support, advice and guidance as required
- safeguard children.

Careful planning is required before children start at a setting. Organising pre-visits helps children to become familiar with the new experience and can ease separation anxiety.

Remember

Make sure rota planning offers consistency and enables key people to 'meet and greet' children and their families. You may devise a back-up key person system so children still enjoy secure relationships when staff are absent.

Childminders

The above guidance applies to childminders who also need to consider:

 EYFS 3.26

In the home environment, the childminder is the key person and the above guidance applies. Pre-visits should also be considered by childminders in order to develop relationships and establish the support children and their families will need in order to feel settled and secure.

Disqualification

➡ EYFS 3.14–EYFS 3.16, CR 2.3 and CR 12.1

If a person becomes disqualified they are no longer able to:

- work in an early years setting
- be involved in the management of an early years setting.

If employers becomes aware of changes in an individual's circumstances that may lead to disqualification, they must act. Employers must safeguard children and no longer employ the individual concerned. In some circumstances, a waiver can be applied for, but the individual must not be employed until a waiver has been granted.

Being a disqualified person has major implication for individuals both professionally and financially. So, some people may choose to conceal this information from their employers. Childminders may choose to conceal this information from Ofsted but failure to notify Ofsted, without a reasonable excuse, is an offence. Effective supervision of staff is crucial in building relationships and part of this is being alert to changes in individuals' circumstances. Make sure staff

Law

Employers need to ensure all staff continue to be suitable to work with children. This includes directors, committee members and ancillary staff. Ensure staff are fully aware of the process regarding suspension and termination of employment contracts. Disqualified people are not permitted to work with children in any capacity. Appealing a disqualification or applying for a waiver does not reinstate their suitability. Written, authorised evidence of a waiver being granted must be in place prior to persons being reinstated.

are aware of the importance of keeping employers informed of any changes in their circumstances that may affect their ongoing suitability.

Informing Ofsted

 EYFS 3.11, EYFS 3.15 and CR 2.3 and CR 12.1

Ofsted must be informed of:

- grounds for disqualification
- relevant dates
- legal details including sentencing information.

A copy of the order must be sent to Ofsted.

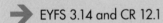 EYFS 3.16

Ofsted must be informed about anything that would jeopardise children's safety as soon as is reasonably practicable, but in any event within 14 days. Ensure all telephone calls are logged, emails are collated and posted documents should be sent recorded delivery as proof of postage.

Law

All details regarding a pending or imposed disqualification must be made to Ofsted. It is an employer's responsibility to ensure all staff are suitable. Therefore, employees need to be fully aware of the implications of becoming a disqualified person.

Law

Individuals need to demonstrate they have contacted Ofsted within 14 days in order to prove they have not committed an offence.

Childminders

The above guidance applies to childminders who also need to consider:

 EYFS 3.14 and CR 12.1

A registered childminder must stop childminding if any or all of the following are deemed disqualified:

- the childminder
- any person living in the same household
- any person employed by the childminder.

! **Remember**

Childminders need to be alert to changes in circumstances of people such as partners, lodgers, children/step children over the age of 16 that may have implications for their registration.

Complaints and inspection

EYFS 3.73, EYFS 3.74 and CR 7.1–CR 7.6

Parents and carers, professionals – indeed any person who is dissatisfied with the quality of childcare provided at a setting – can make a complaint. Sometimes, this can be resolved amicably, without Ofsted becoming involved. Providers must enable parents and carers to escalate their concerns by providing contact information for Ofsted.

Ofsted will not investigate complaints about contractual, business disputes or fee structures. Ofsted's response to concerns being raised is to ensure all providers are adhering to their conditions of registration and meeting the requirements of the EYFS. This may be ascertained by an inspection. Ofsted risk assess complaint information and decide how quickly an inspection is required. A full inspection report is published following an inspection. For more information see 'Conducting priority and brought forward inspections following risk assessment' (July 2013). http://www.ofsted.gov.uk/resources/conducting-priority-and-brought-forward-inspections-following-risk-assessment.

Complaints can be malicious and can arise from disgruntled service users, disputes with neighbours or ex-staff. Ineffective communication systems and contractual disputes tend to underpin most malicious complaints.

Law

Inspections are conducted under sections 49 and 50 of the Childcare Act 2006. This legislation covers the period from the inspection to the publication of the report.

Remember

It is crucial that you foster professional relationships with parents and/or carers, especially regarding exchanging information and having a clear fee structure.

All providers registered with Ofsted will be subject to inspection. This is to ensure compliance with the EYFS. Parents and carers must have access to a copy of the inspection report. Providers will be inspected at least once in each cycle or more frequently if concerns are raised. From November 2013, the gradings are: outstanding (1), good (2), requires improvement (3) and inadequate (4). For more information on how inspections are graded see 'Evaluation schedule for inspections of registered early years provision' (October 2013). http://www.ofsted.gov.uk/resources/evaluation-schedule-for-inspections-of-registered-early-years-provision.

Each inspection conducted is unique, based on the evidence provided on the day. Therefore, inspection gradings are not pre-empted, not guaranteed and may change from previous inspections, based on the day's findings. From November, 2013, the focus of inspection is safeguarding, teaching and safety. 'Teaching' is a broad term and encompasses many elements, including how well children learn, develop and the importance of children's emotional well-being. For more information on preparation for inspection see; 'Are you ready for your inspection? A guide to inspections of provision on Ofsted's Childcare and Early Years Registers' (August 2012). http://www.ofsted.gov.uk/resources/are-you-ready-for-your-inspection-guide-inspections-of-provision-ofsteds-childcare-and-early-years-r.

Providers must demonstrate how they comply with the EYFS and show evidence of their own evaluation of their provision. For more information on self-evaluation see http://www.ofsted.gov.uk/resources/early-years-online-self-evaluation-form-sef-and-guidance-for-providers-delivering-early-years-founda.

Written procedures

➡ EYFS 3.73 and CR 7.1

Providers must have clear procedures for dealing with all complaints and concerns. Detailed complaint records must be in place and include investigation details and outcomes.

➡ EYFS CR 7.2, CR 7.4, CR 7.5, CR 7.6

A 28-day timescale is stipulated to investigate and resolve internal complaints and information relating to complaints must be made available to Ofsted on request.

The Childcare Register stipulates that complaints records must be kept for three years.

➡ EYFS 3.74 and CR 9.3

Contact details for Ofsted must be made available within settings in order for parents and carers or other service users to escalate concerns they may have about the setting's compliance with the EYFS. Notifications of Ofsted inspections (if known) and the final Ofsted report must be made available to parents and carers.

Childminders

The above guidance applies to childminders who also need to consider:

➡ EYFS 3.73

The EYFS states there is no requirement for childminders to have a written complaints procedure. However, if a childminder is registered on the Childcare Register, under CR 7.1 it outlines that 'Childminders must have a written statement of procedures to be followed in relation to complaints which relate to the requirements of the Childcare Register and which a parent makes in writing or by email'. Therefore, if you are registered on the childcare register a robust, written complaints procedure is required.

Changes that must be notified to Ofsted

➡ EYFS 3.76, EYFS 3.77 and CR 10, CR 11, CR 12.1, CR 12.2, CR 12.3, CR 13

As a registered provider, you must inform Ofsted of changes that may affect your registration such as:

- change in address, including if you move premises or rooms to part of a building not previously registered
- change of hours; if you change your hours of operation, such as opening at 7am instead of 8am or if you decide to offer overnight care
- changes affecting space or quality. If you alter your building, such as adding an extension or erecting dividing walls in rooms, or if

you relocate age groups of children to different locations (such as moving a baby room from downstairs to upstairs) then these types of changes may have implications for the numbers of children you may care for and the quality of the environment

- details of the provider, such as if the registered person moves house, changes to contact information, such as phone numbers.
- change of manager; if you have significant staff changes to the management team
- significant event; anything that would affect an individual's suitability such as involvement with police or social services
- change to company or charity name or number, or any business changes such as re-naming or re-registering a business
- nominated person change; this includes individuals or changes within groups that are registered
- changes to partners, governing body such as new directors or new committee members must be notified.

(Ofsted factsheet: 'Records, policies and notification requirements of the Early Years Register', January 2013)

 EYFS 3.77

All relevant information must be provided to Ofsted. This includes any new names, former names, and any aliases, date of birth and home address details. You may be asked to produce evidence of your notifications to Ofsted, so ensure you keep records of phone calls, emails, letters and so on as if you cannot demonstrate that you have informed Ofsted of significant changes within 14 days, you may have committed an offence.

 Law

You must notify changes within 14 days. Failure to do so is an offence.

Employers' duties to their employees

 Health & Safety at Work etc. Act 1974 (HSWA) Section 2(1)

The Health and Safety at Work Etc. Act 1974 places a general duty on an employer to ensure, so far is reasonably practicable, the health safety and welfare of their employees at work.

 HSWA 1974 Section 2(2)

This very general duty divides into a number of more specific ones, which stipulate the principles of running a safe workplace:

- provide safe equipment and maintain it in a safe condition
- provide safe working procedures
- make arrangements to use, handle, store, move and transport articles and substances safely
- provide information, instruction training and supervision
- provide a safe place to work including access to and from the workplace
- provide a healthy environment, including arrangements for welfare facilities.

Do you have in place:

- a system to purchase, check and maintain equipment?
- well-understood and established safety procedures?
- trained staff who understand their job responsibilities and follow your safety procedures?
- a system for identifying, reporting and dealing with defects or problems in the workplace?
- welfare facilities, for example toilets, hot water, ventilation, lighting etc?

Childminders

 HSWA 1974 Section 3(2)

Self-employed people also have a duty to themselves to conduct their business in such a manner that they do not expose themselves to risks to their own health and safety.

Employers' duties to people not in their employment

 HSWA 1974 Section 3(1)

It shall be the duty of every employer to conduct his undertaking in such a way as to ensure, so far as is reasonably practicable, that persons not in his employment who may be affected thereby are not thereby exposed to risks to their health or safety.

The employer must consider other people who are not their employees but may be affected by the running of the business. Therefore, as an employer you must consider other people who are not your staff but who use, visit, or work in your establishment:

- children in your care
- your visitors, for example, parents, delivery drivers, registration officers
- contractors or workmen working at your premises, for example, window cleaner.

Ask yourself:

- Have I considered these people in my safety procedures and risk assessments?
- How could these people get hurt?
- Do I have any controls in place to prevent this from happening?
- Are staff aware of these controls?
- Do staff follow these controls in practice?
- Is there anything else that I need to do?

 Law

'So far as is reasonably practicable' qualifies the health and safety duties and has its basis in case law. It is also implied in health and safety regulation, particularly in relation to risk assessment, requiring you to assess what needs to be done by looking at risk versus the sacrifice.

If the likelihood of someone getting hurt and the severity of the injury is grossly disproportionate to the cost of dealing with the risk, then the risk is significant and action must be taken to reduce the risk to the lowest possible level.

Equally, if the risk is insignificant in relation to the cost, then it is not reasonably practicable to undertake the work. Risk assessment requires you to consider this prior to an accident or incident occurring.

HSE provides guidance regarding this concept at http://www.hse.gov.uk/risk/theory/alarpglance.htm.

Risk assessment is discussed in Chapter 7.

Health and safety policy

 HSWA 1974 Section 2(3)

An employer has to prepare and revise when necessary a written statement of their general policy with respect to the general health and safety of their employees and the organisation and arrangements to carry out that policy effectively.

The policy and any revisions must be brought to the attention of employees.

What should be included in a health and safety policy

You must set out what you want to achieve in terms of health and safety. This is called your **statement of intent**, in which you think about your objectives and what your commitment to health and safety is.

Organisation: you must state who is responsible for tasks, by either job description or name. Staff must know what their responsibilities are and, critically, have information, instruction, training and supervision to help them to do their job properly.

Arrangements: these are the procedures/precautions in place to secure health and safety in the premises and in the activities that take place in your business.

This policy statement should:

- be signed by the person in overall charge, for example, the employer
- be dated and it is good practice to include a future date for revision.

You need to bring the policy and any revisions to the attention of your employees. It will only be effective if it is a working document used by management and staff.

Many of the best policies are where staff have been actively involved in helping to identify what needs to be done and how to do it.

 Law

Under health and safety law if you employ fewer than five people your health and safety policy does not have to be in writing, but you still need to have a policy on health and safety. It is a good idea to have some documented policies and procedures. This is a requirement under the EYFS.

Remember

In an inspection, or investigation or complaint situation the health and safety policy and procedures may be examined to evaluate what should happen relative to what has happened. Enforcement officers may also question you and your staff to determine knowledge of responsibilities, policies and procedures relevant to the role.

HSE provides information about writing a health and safety policy and a simple model template, which can be adapted to reflect the complexity of your business. An example of a completed health and safety policy is also available at http://www.hse.gov.uk/contact/faqs/policy.htm.

Employers' duties to consult with employees

➡ The Health & Safety (Consultation with Employees) Regulations 1996 (as amended) Regulation 3

The law relating to the provision of a health and safety policy recognises the importance of bringing the employees' attention to both the policy and any revisions.

Other specific regulations are in place requiring an employer to consult with their employees on health and safety matters and to provide them with information regarding risks to their health and safety.

HSE has produced a leaflet on consulting with employees; 'Consulting employees on health and safety a brief guide to the law' available at http://www.hse.gov.uk/pubns/indg232.pdf.

➡ The Health and Safety (Information for Employees) Regulations 1989 (as amended) Regulation 4

These regulations require you to provide information to employees. This may be done by displaying the 'Health and Safety Law Poster' or providing your employees with the equivalent pocket card or leaflet.

The 1999 poster or leaflet must be replaced with the 2009 poster or leaflet no later than 5 April 2014.

Inspection and enforcement

➡ HSWA 1974 Section 18

Every workplace may receive an inspection/intervention to assess that the employer/self-employed person is meeting their responsibilities under the Health and Safety at Work Etc. Act 1974 and other health and safety regulations.

A health and safety inspector may visit your premises in a number of circumstances including these situations:

- to carry out a routine inspection
- to investigate a complaint
- to investigate an accident or certain types of work related illness
- other intervention such as information gathering.

As a result of an inspection, the enforcing authority will make an assessment giving the business a risk rating. This will determine the frequency of future inspections, based on the management control of risk.

Enforcing authorities have enforcement policies and work programmes, detailing what they do and how they will achieve their targets. HSE has produced the National Local Authority Enforcement Code. This is a statutory code for local authorities regulators. This code came into effect on 29 May 2013. Work programmes need to reflect the guidance in this code. In future proactive health and safety inspections will be focused on high-risk activities in certain sectors. They may also be based on intelligence such as complaints.

The code and a list of high-risk activities and sectors is available on HSE's website at http://www.hse.gov.uk/lau/publications/la-enforcement-code.htm?ebul=hsegen&cr=2/3-june-13.

The hazard of the infection of children with e.coli or cryptosporidium from open farm or animal visitor attractions visits, where there is a lack of suitable control measures, is listed as a suitable target for proactive inspection.

> **Childminders**
>
> As a self-employed person your home, or workplace, that you use for your business, may be subject to an inspection.

Enforcing authorities

In the United Kingdom, there are two bodies responsible for enforcing health and safety laws. They are:

- Health and Safety Executive (HSE), a government-based organisation
- Environmental health practitioners/officers/technical officers in local government organisations such as local councils and often called the local authority (LA).

There is a set of regulations that detail which enforcing authority deals with types of premises. In childcare responsibility is split.

Guidance can be obtained from HSE's website at http://www.hse.gov.uk/foi/internalops/fod/oc/100-199/124-11-appendix.htm.

If you are in any doubt which body is your 'enforcing authority', your local Environmental Health Department will help you.

Enforcement powers

 HSWA 1974 Sections 19 and 20

Enforcement officers are available for advice and guidance. Officers will be appointed and may be authorised with powers such as:

- a right of entry at all reasonable times
- stopping activities if there is a risk of serious personal injury
- taking enforcement action, for example issuing letters, serving notices and initiating prosecution proceedings
- investigating the workplace, asking questions
- to inspect, seize and copy documents
- to dismantle and remove equipment
- to take photos and samples.

All inspectors will carry identification and authorisation that you can verify.

A leaflet explaining what to expect when an inspector visits your business is available from HSE's website at http://www.hse.gov.uk/pubns/hsc14.pdf.

Enforcement outcomes

Post inspection or investigation a variety of enforcement outcomes may be applied by an enforcement officer dependent upon the outcome of the inspection/visit and the nature of the health and safety breach. Major non-compliance with the laws are usually dealt with formally through the service of a statutory notice.

A statutory notice is a legal document, which specifies the law that has been breached, the officer's opinion and reason for serving the notice. It tells you what needs to be done and gives a specific time limit to do the work. There are two types of statutory notice that can be served.

- **Improvement notice**

This notice requires you to do the specified remedial work in a timescale that is at least 21 days. This type of notice could be served for a problem, such as an uneven floor covering providing a tripping hazard or the lack of a handrail on stairs.

- **Prohibition notice**

This notice is served when there is a very serious breach that results, or could result, in a risk of serious personal injury. The notice will again specify what is wrong and what remedial action needs to be taken. The notice can stop any activity immediately or after a specified period of time. For example, a notice could be served if an external play area was contaminated with glass or if the equipment was dangerous.

In both of these cases you can appeal to an Employment Tribunal if you think the notice is unfair and details are given on the notice of how to do this. There is a strict time limit for appeal that will be detailed on the notice. You are committing an offence if you fail to comply with an improvement notice or a prohibition notice.

If you appeal against an improvement notice, the work required by the notice is suspended until the appeal is determined. However, you must comply with a prohibition notice even if you have appealed against it. The outcome will be determined at the appeal.

- **Prosecution**

This action is taken where there have been very serious breaches of health and safety laws. These may have resulted in a fatality or a serious injury. Companies and individuals, including employees, may be prosecuted under the Health and Safety at Work etc. Act 1974. A prosecution can take place in addition to the service of enforcement notices.

In recent years, there have been a number of prosecutions taken against employers in the childcare sector for fatalities and serious injuries to children in their care. In certain exceptional circumstances, an alternative to prosecution can be the issue of a simple caution (previously known as a formal caution).

Strict criteria and guidance are in place and enforcement officers must consider these when deciding upon enforcement outcomes. This will be detailed in the enforcing authority's enforcement policy and is available from the authority.

Remember

Both HSE and the local authorities have procedures in place for receiving and dealing with complaints. If you believe you have been treated unfairly or are dissatisfied with the inspection outcome, you can make a complaint to the authority.

2 Employee responsibilities

The EYFS section of this chapter covers the organisation of childcare, managing children's behaviour, equal opportunities. Managing behaviour sensitively, consistently and appropriately to children's age and stage of development requires experience and training. Meeting children's individual needs requires professional, dedicated staff who recognise children's uniqueness and celebrates difference. Inclusion needs to underpin all aspects of practice in order for children to reach their full potential and feel valued.

There are clearly defined responsibilities for both employers and employees under the Health and Safety at Work Etc. Act 1974. These duties include a responsibility on the employee to take reasonable care of their own health and safety and others affected by their actions and to cooperate with the employer on health and safety matters. The Management of Health and Safety at Work Regulations 1999 also place an emphasis on training and instruction given to employees by their employer to enable them to fulfil their responsibilities.

Managing behaviour, policies and procedures

 EYFS 3.50, CR 6.2 and CR 6.3

Staff must be conversant with policies and procedures relating to behaviour management. There must be a named person responsible for behaviour management. This person needs to be competent in dealing with different behaviours, liaising with children's families and professionals. The named person needs to enable and support the staff team in dealing with challenging behaviour.

Be alert to influences in a child's life that may have an impact on their behaviour such as:

- child's age and stage of development
- communication difficulties, speech or hearing, resulting in frustration
- an underlying condition, such as autism
- violence and physical abuse within the home
- sexual abuse
- emotional abuse
- bullying
- poverty
- family breakdown, divorce, separation
- birth of a baby
- death of a family member.

Managing a mixed age range

 EYFS 3.50 and CR 6.3

Sharing can pose difficulties for younger children and older children may become frustrated with younger children's behaviour. Consider the impact of how well younger and older children integrate and play together. All children's needs must be planned for and behaviour dealt with according to their age and stage of development.

Remember

Effective use of the progress check for two-year-olds should detect early any problems in a child's development or special educational needs. For more information see 'A Know How Guide. The EYFS progress check at age two'. https://www.education.gov.uk/publications/.../NCB-00087-2012.

Adults play a crucial role in helping children to be responsible for their own behaviour and laying the foundations of positive social interactions. Adults need to adopt positive behaviour management strategies. Using different communication methods, such as signing and 'Makaton' can help younger children communicate their needs and feelings, thus avoiding frustration which can then escalate into disruptive behaviour.

Other strategies include:

- being a good role model and adopting a calm, patient disposition
- having realistic expectations
- being consistent in delivering strategies, utilising experience and updating training
- being clear about boundaries and consequences, avoiding provocation and escalation
- praising positive behaviour and effort
- helping children reflect on their behaviour, for example, how it feels to share toys and help them to develop empathy.

Corporal punishment

 EYFS 3.51, EYFS 3.52, CR 1.4 and CR 1.5

Corporal punishment is defined as any physical punishment to deliberately inflict pain, such as smacking or caning to enforce discipline. Under the EYFS, no person is allowed to inflict or threaten corporal punishment on a child and must protect children from any person who attempts to discipline children in this way.

Physical intervention can be used if a child is in immediate danger to themselves, others or property. Policies and procedures must be explicit about when physical intervention could be used in order to promote consistency and clarity across the staff team.

Remember

There is a difference between physical intervention and corporal punishment. Ensure staff are very clear about the distinction and their duty to record all incidents where physical intervention is used.

Equal opportunities

 EYFS 3.66, CR 6.4 and CR 6.5

Every setting must have policies and procedures outlining how equality of opportunity is to be promoted. Equality is not about treating everyone the same, it is recognising and valuing differences and tailoring individual care and education accordingly.

This involves:

- following children's interests
- adapting the environment
- using a multi-sensory approach
- helping children make links in their learning.

 Remember

The four overarching principles of the EYFS must underpin and shape your practice:

- Unique child.
- Positive relationships.
- Enabling environments.
- Children developing and learning at different rates in different ways.

SENCO

 EYFS 3.66 and EYFS 3.72, CR 6.4 and CR 6.5

Children who are disabled or have special educational needs must be fully included in all aspects of your setting. There must be an appointed Special Educational Needs Coordinator (SENCO) in group provision to coordinate, evaluate and monitor inclusion. This is a skilled role and requires training and specialist knowledge in order to fully support all children, their families and the staff team.

A SENCO should:

- coordinate additional support
- assess the child's needs and set targets for improvement
- overcome barriers to a child's learning
- request the involvement of other professionals
- liaise with families, schools and other external services.

Support services may be provided by:

- a speech and language therapist (SaLT)
- an occupational therapist (OT) or
- specialist advisory services dealing with autism or behavioural needs
- educational psychologist.

The prime areas of learning and development are fundamental throughout the EYFS. From November 2013, inspections will be more focused on the impact of teaching on all children's education and their personal and emotional development. For guidance on child development, see 'Early years outcomes' (September 2013). https://www.gov.uk/government/publications/early-years-outcomes.

 Remember

Communication and language is a prime area of learning and development. For more advice on children's language development see http:// www.literacytrust.org.uk/early_years.

Evaluation procedures

 EYFS 3.66

It is important to evaluate inclusive practice on an ongoing basis in order to ensure children's needs are consistently met. This also helps to identify:

- priorities
- refine development plans
- balance intervention strategies and encourage child-initiated learning.

Different local authorities may offer an audit tool to help focus the evaluation. A 360° degree approach is imperative to ascertain crucial information to influence change. Involving all parties ensures people's experiences are shared and their opinions valued. Ensure you involve:

- adults (staff, students, apprentices, volunteers)
- children
- parents and carers
- professionals.

Children's feedback can be enlightening in its honesty and clarity. Therefore, be creative about the systems you use for gathering feedback from children.

Think about using:

- puppets
- role play
- art materials
- digital cameras
- happy/sad face stickers.

Challenging inappropriate attitudes and practice

 EYFS 3.66, CR 6.4 and CR 6.5

Children learn through play and are influenced by their home circumstances, community and media in developing their understanding about society. Children can behave in discriminatory ways, such as name calling, teasing or excluding certain children based on their experience and influences. Staff must be alert to such incidents and challenge accordingly. This requires sensitivity to ensure children can understand, think about and change their behaviour.

If a situation arises, staff need to:

- intervene, but do not ignore, condone or make excuses for a child
- be precise, specific and clear when explaining to a child why you have intervened
- help children empathise, and ask them how would they feel
- encourage apologies
- support all children in moving forward.

Staff are also influenced by their home circumstances, community and media and bring their own value system to the workplace. It is important to challenge adults if their practice is inappropriate, such as attitudes towards certain children, comments and innuendos. Sometimes staff may continually underestimate children's abilities, particularly children with learning difficulties and special educational needs. Regular supervision is imperative to ensure staff can share any concerns about their own or colleagues practice.

Challenging parents and carers about inappropriate comments or attitudes requires assertiveness, discretion and respect. Adults may have an engrained value and belief system, be resistant to change and offended by (and perceive) your challenge as confrontation.

Information leaflets, training workshops, outside speakers outlining the effects of prejudice, discrimination and bullying on a child can help to educate parents and carers and in turn get them to reflect on their belief systems.

 Law

The Children and Families Bill 2013 section on Special educational needs (SEN) reflects a new approach to special educational needs and disability. Key components encompass early identification and assessment with a new birth-to-25 education, health and care plan, giving parents control through personal budgets and improving cooperation between all the services by requiring them to work together for children and their families. For more information see 'Children and Families Bill 2013' (October 2013); http://www.education.gov.uk/a00221161/.

 Remember

Bullying, teasing and harassment cause emotional hurt, including damaged self-confidence, self-image and self-esteem.

Childminders

The above guidance applies to childminders who also need to consider:

 EYFS 3.50, CR 1.4 and CR 1.5

The childminder is responsible for managing children's behaviour appropriately. Any situations where physical intervention is used must be recorded. Childminders have a duty to protect children from any adults within the household who may want to use corporal punishment on childminded children.

Employee responsibilities – health and safety

 Health & Safety at Work etc. Act 1974 (HSWA) Section 7

Employees at work also have responsibilities to:

- take reasonable care of their own health and safety and of other people who may be affected by their actions at work
- cooperate with their employer or other people who have responsibility under health and safety laws, to enable the duty holder to comply with the law.

Employees must also cooperate with you in health and safety matters, for example by:

- following the safety procedures that you have in place
- notifying accidents to the responsible person
- using any personal protective equipment that is provided for health and safety purposes.

 HSWA 1974 Section 8

An employee must not misuse or interfere with anything provided for the purposes of health and safety.

 HSWA 1974 Sections 33 (1)(a) and 33 (1)(b)

An employee can be prosecuted as an individual if they fail to comply with their duty under Section 7 and/or contravene the requirement of Section 8 of the Act.

Cooperating with the employer and following health and safety precautions is a theme that runs through other health and safety regulations, such as the Manual Handling Operations Regulations 1992 (as amended) which require employees to follow appropriate procedures laid down by the employer and to promote the safe handling of loads.

 The Management of Health and Safety at Work Regulations 1999 Regulation 14

These regulations place duties on an employee to:

- use work equipment properly and in accordance with the training and instructions given by the employer
- to inform their employer or any person appointed by their employer to assist in health and safety matters of any situation at work that is dangerous.

You must have a system in place to enable the reporting of any health and safety problems to the responsible person, enabling corrective action to be taken.

It is also critical that staff fully understand their responsibilities and what is expected of them. They cannot achieve this unless the employer has met their responsibilities.

 Remember

Challenging and dealing with unsafe behaviour is an important part of health and safety management.

 Law

Prosecution of an individual may take place where a serious risk or breach of the law is identified, for example after a serious accident or incident. This action would be considered where the individual had shown a reckless disregard for health and safety, exposing themselves or others to serious risk of injury.

3 Suitable and 'competent persons'

The EYFS outlines considerations for assessing the suitability of individuals. This chapter examines the requirement to provide suitable people in a setting, looking at recruitment and ongoing suitability. It also provides guidance regarding staff taking medication and other substances.

The Management of Health and Safety at Work Regulations 1999 require an employer to appoint a competent person(s) to assist in meeting their health and safety responsibilities, including risk assessment. The theme of 'competent person' runs through all the risk based health and safety laws where assessment of risks is required.

Systems to assess suitability

➡ EYFS 3.9–EYFS 3.13, CR 2.3 and CR 3

Being deemed 'suitable to work with children' involves:

- completing an honest, accurate application form
- providing a full, complete career history
- being able to supply appropriate references
- being deemed healthy and fit to work with children
- being willing to undergo suitability checks, such as DBS
- being qualified and experienced in or be willing to work towards a relevant qualification
- be willing to undertake further ongoing training.

Evaluate your suitability systems:

- Do you follow published guidance, such as 'Working together to safeguard children' (DFE 2013), 'Helping employers make safer recruiting decisions' (DBS 2013), Ofsted Factsheet: 'Childcare – Disclosure and Barring Service (DBS) checks for those providers who register with Ofsted' (Ofsted 2013) and adopt a proper application and selection procedures?
- Do you obtain enhanced DBS disclosures and the associated identity checks, including compliance with the Disclosure and Barring Service guidance?
- Do you obtain details of employment history, references and any other necessary checks, such as an employee's physical and mental health?
- How do you ensure all your staff continue to be suitable?

Remember

All staff working with children are required to deliver learning and development requirements of the EYFS (unless you have been granted an exemption). For information relating to exemptions see: http://www.ofsted.gov.uk/resources/factsheet-childcare-registration-and-inspection-of-providers-who-hold-exemptions-learning-and-developement-requirements.

Disclosure and Barring Service (DBS) checks

 EYFS 3.10 and EYFS 3.12, CR 2.3 and CR 3

The Criminal Records Bureau (CRB) and the Independent Safeguarding Authority (ISA) have merged into the Disclosure and Barring Service (DBS).

DBS checks are undertaken in order to establish if a person:

- has a criminal conviction or caution that will disqualify them from registering as a childcare provider
- is barred from working with children
- has any other convictions, cautions, reprimands or warnings that would give rise to a cause for concern about them working with children.

Disqualification

 EYFS 3.14–EYFS 3.16 and CR 12.1

Some people are disqualified from providing, or working in, registered early years provision and childcare. A person who is disqualified is not allowed to:

- provide, or be directly concerned in the management of, any registered childminding or childcare service
- register, manage, have a financial interest in or be employed at a children's home
- foster a child privately.

You will need to declare all issues relating to your family circumstances both currently and in the past. Problems such as domestic violence, substance misuse, mental illness and criminal behaviour and any convictions may have an effect on your suitability. A full list of all the circumstances that disqualify people from working with children is available in The Childcare (Disqualification) Regulations 2009, available from: www.opsi.gov.uk/si/si2009/uksi_20091547_en_1.

Law

Ofsted cannot register or allow registration to continue where people are disqualified by law from registration. It is an offence for someone registered to provide childminding or childcare to knowingly employ someone who is disqualified.

Law

The Childcare (Early Years Register) Regulations 2008 Schedule 2, 8, 11 and 12 (a) and (b) place a duty on the registered person of childcare on non-domestic premises to have systems in place to undertake background checks and make suitability decisions for childcare staff and those living or working on childcare premises other than the manager.

! Remember

You are also disqualified if you live in the same household as another person who is disqualified, or fits the criteria for disqualification or if you live in a household where a disqualified person is employed.

Disqualified people may, in some circumstances, apply to Ofsted for a decision to waive their disqualification. Ofsted consider each request on its own merits taking into account the reasons for the disqualification, the length of time of disqualification and the risk to children. Ofsted will assess your request and notify you in writing of their decision.

Disclosure and change of circumstances

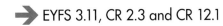 EYFS 3.11, CR 2.3 and CR 12.1

All staff, students, apprentices and volunteers must be clear about your setting's policy on disclosure. Devise a self-disclosure form that encompasses the following:

- convictions
- change in family circumstances (for example, domestic violence)
- cautions
- court orders
- reprimands
- warnings.

 Remember

Staff must disclose information relating to any of the above received before or during employment at the setting.

Vetting process

 EYFS 3.10–EYFS 3.13, CR 2.3 and CR 3

The registered person must ensure that no individual who is unsuitable to work with children has unsupervised access to a child receiving childcare. Providers must ensure that a relevant audit trail of all suitability decisions is evidenced, such as verification of identity and staff qualifications. You need to record DBS disclosure reference numbers, dates of disclosure and who obtained the disclosure. These processes must be robust. The serious case review into a nursery where children were abused by a predatory paedophile employed by the setting highlights how imperative rigorous recruitment procedures are in place and adhered to by recommending, 'Effective recruitment processes that move beyond a focus on CRB checks to an exploration of motivation and value base. This will give a clear message to potential staff that abuse will not be tolerated' (Wonnacott, J. 2013, p8. Serious case review case No.2010–11/3).

When judging the effectiveness of governance and leadership of the early year's provision, inspectors will take into consideration different elements. These include the effectiveness of arrangements for safeguarding, including recruitment practices and how well safe practices and a culture of safety are promoted and understood. Inspectors will need reassurance that there are no gaps in your vetting processes or breaches of your recruitment policy.

Safeguarding Vulnerable Groups Act 2006

 EYFS 3.13, CR 2.3

The Safeguarding Vulnerable Groups Act 2006 was passed as a result of the Bichard Inquiry (HMSO 2004) arising from the Soham murders in 2002. The Inquiry questioned the way employers recruit people to work with vulnerable groups, and particularly the way background checks are carried out.

 Remember

Ensure you and your staff are aware of your responsibilities under the Safeguarding Vulnerable Groups Act 2006. You can access the legislation at http://www.legislation.gov.uk.

Staff taking medication and other substances

 EYFS 3.17, CR 1.8

You must ensure that no one smokes, or consumes, or is under the influence of, drugs (including medication that may have an adverse effect on the individual's ability to provide childcare) or alcohol on the premises at any time while childcare is provided, or in the presence of a child receiving childcare. The use of some substances, though not illegal, may affect a person's suitability to look after, or be in contact with, young children. These include glue sniffing or misuse of other legal substances such as solvents or lighter fuel, and addiction to prescription drugs, or even drugs that can be bought 'over the counter', such as painkillers.

 Remember

An inspector is required to ask about weekly drinking patterns as part of a registration visit, even when there is no obvious concern about alcohol misuse. If inspectors are concerned about a person's suitability they will refer their concerns to Ofsted.

Providers must be aware of signs potential substance misuse including:

- appearance of the member of staff, such as personal hygiene, smell of alcohol, sores or spots around the mouth
- erratic, delusional or paranoid behaviour, secretiveness, inability to focus, mood changes, loud, obnoxious behaviour or laughing at nothing
- incoherent speech, abnormal speed, making endless excuses
- signs of intoxication or dependency, track marks on legs or arms, lack of coordination and balance, flushed cheeks, dilated pupils, appearance of unusual containers or wrappers and drug apparatus on the premises.

(Ofsted: Registration and suitability handbook, 2012)

You must adopt robust policies and procedures for dealing with staff who you suspect of potential substance misuse. Your first priority must be to assess the risk to children. You must take appropriate action to investigate the concerns, where necessary suspending staff until investigations are complete.

Remember

You must inform Ofsted of any substance misuse investigation results. Ofsted may need to make an assessment about the continued suitability of the childcare provider.

If concerns are escalated to Ofsted, a medical officer is appointed who will carry out a full review of all information and make the decision based on:

- the accuracy of the self-declaration
- information from checks from other sources including from the inspector
- appropriate additional tests or medical interviews from a range of sources.

Substance misuse problems (including alcohol) are dealt with by the Community Drug Team. That team is led by a consultant psychiatrist, who will be supported by community psychiatric nurses, counsellors, drug workers and psychologists. Where it is deemed children are at risk of serious harm the Compliance, Investigation and Enforcement Team of Ofsted will consider suspension and/or emergency cancellation of registration.

Law

Where a childcare provider commits or is committing an offence under the Misuse of Drugs Act 1971, this will raise issues about their suitability to remain qualified as a registered provider.

The Act classifies drugs according to the degree of harm likely to be involved in their use, i.e. Class A, B or C.

- Class A – Ecstasy, LSD, heroin, cocaine, crack, magic mushrooms, amphetamines (if prepared for injection).
- Class B – Amphetamines, Methylphenidate (Ritalin), Pholcodine.
- Class C – Cannabis, tranquilisers, some painkillers, Gamma hydroxybutyrate (GHB), Ketamine.

For more information on suitability refer to http://www.ofsted.gov.uk/resources/registration-and-suitability-handbook.

Childminders

The above guidance applies to childminders who also need to consider:

 CR 1.9 VCR

Home childcarers must not smoke, or consume or be under the influence of drugs (including medication that may have an adverse effect on their ability to provide childcare) or alcohol while providing childcare.

Household members' behaviour can have a major impact on a childminders or assistant's ongoing suitability. Always seek advice if anyone in the house hold over the age of 16 becomes involved with the police, social services or develops serious health issues.

'Competent persons'

→ The Management of Health and Safety at Work Regulations 1999 Regulation 7(1)

Every employer shall appoint a 'competent person(s)' to assist in health and safety matters.

This person can be:

- you or your business partner, or
- a business employee, or
- someone from outside the business under contract for assistance.

Whoever it is, they must be competent.

What is competence?

Competence is not specifically defined in regulations. It is a combination of a number of factors:

- knowledge and experience of the workplace and the tasks undertaken there
- personal qualities, such as good communication, listening, observation skills; knowing personal limitations
- training or an understanding of best practice, knowledge of where to look for information and how to apply it.

To appoint a 'competent person', an employer needs to understand their own business and associated risks. If the business is complex with high-risk levels, your 'competent person' will require a higher level of skills to assist you properly.

Appointing a 'competent person'

→ The Management of Health and Safety at Work Regulations 1999 Regulation 7(8)

Where the employer employs a person(s) in the business who is considered to be competent, then the law encourages that such an employee from the workforce should be appointed in preference to an external person from outside of the organisation.

- talk to staff and tell them that you need to appoint someone to help you
- ask yourself whether any of the staff have the skills to fulfil this role and would like to do it
- if you are not confident, then consider getting help from outside of the business to provide this assistance
- you can appoint someone to help, advise and support both you and your competent member of staff.

HSE holds a register of Occupational Safety and Health Consultants (OSHCR) at http://www.hse.gov.uk/oshcr/index.htm.

If you appoint a consultant, ask to see evidence of their qualifications, continuous professional development and details of their experience, such as curriculum vitae, references or testimonials from other business clients.

 The Management of Health and Safety at Work Regulations 1999 Regulations 7(3) and 7(4)

Any 'competent person' appointed needs sufficient time to do this job. This person must have an understanding of your business and you must cooperate with them. Understanding the business is particularly important if you appoint a 'competent person' externally.

Childminders

→ The Management of Health and Safety at Work Regulations 1999 Regulation 7(6)

If you are self-employed you may act in this role provided you are competent to do it.

 Law

Appointing a 'competent person' is a requirement that runs through other regulations requiring the assessment of risk, for example fire safety law.

4 Training

Training is an essential element of any business operation. 'The biggest influence on the quality of early education and care is its workforce. Those who engage with children, supporting their learning and interaction with their environment through play, can affect their well-being, development and achievements. When we talk about the 'quality' of staff, their qualifications are key' (p15, Nutbrown Review 2012; 'Foundations for quality. The independent review of early education and childcare qualifications. Final Report').

The EYFS outlines qualification levels, the requirements for the manager's role and deputy with regard to taking overall charge of the setting and to meet the leadership and management requirements. This chapter includes referring to the www.education.gov.uk website to ensure qualifications are included in the required framework.

The Health and Safety at Work etc. Act 1974 is explicit regarding an employer's responsibilities to provide information, instruction, training and supervision. This requirement is also present in regulations, such as the Management of Health and Safety at Work Regulations 1999.

Staff need to be provided with information, instruction, training and supervision. An employer also needs to provide a conducive learning environment to develop their skills. This includes:

- identifying training needs
- planning and implementation to meet needs
- assessing the successfulness of training by outcomes in the workplace
- reviewing to identify any further needs or gaps.

These essential requirements help to develop and maintain a professional workforce.

Appropriate qualifications

→ EYFS 1.12, EYFS 3.18–EYFS 3.25, CR 4.3 and CR 4.4

The EYFS highlights the importance of all staff having the appropriate levels of knowledge, skills, clear roles and responsibilities. In response to the Nutbrown Review (2012) and the publication of 'More great childcare: raising quality and giving parents more choice' (2013). The government has introduced new policy: 'Improving the quality and range of education and childcare from birth to 5 years' (2013). This means childcare qualifications are undergoing significant changes. The aim is to build on the Early Years Professional Status (EYPS) programme by introducing early years teachers and early years educators to further improvement quality and outcomes for children. For more information see https://www.gov.uk/government/news/childcare-qualifications-overhaul. The Qualification Database Approved List at http://www.education.gov.uk, is a researchable resource that contains all approved early years and childcare qualifications. There are currently 76 approved level 3 qualifications listed.

Induction

 EYFS 3.18, CR 4.3 and CR 4.4

A well-planned, well-organised induction is the key to the successful integration of new staff, students, apprentices and volunteers into your setting. Induction needs to happen on day one and is the first step of any training programme.

It helps to:

- build on initial enthusiasm, motivation and positive attitudes
- helps to reduce the stress of starting a new job or placement
- be a starting point for CPD
- may help to reduce staff sickness levels and ultimately help to retain professional staff.

The EYFS outlines certain elements that must be included in induction:

- emergency evacuation procedures
- safeguarding
- child protection
- equality
- health and safety.

In addition to the above list, it is helpful to consider including:

- first day information to help staff feel welcome, such as the location of staff room and toilets
- administrative and personnel processes, like signing-in and out systems, rotas, contact numbers
- the terms and conditions of employment contracts and your setting's code of conduct.

The induction process is crucial in helping to safeguard children. You must ensure new staff, students, apprentices and volunteers are given information regarding:

Policies and procedures

- safeguarding and child protection
- behaviour management, physical intervention or restraint
- intimate care
- internet safety
- mobile phones and images
- local safeguarding children's board information
- anti-bullying policy
- anti-racism policy.

Conduct and behaviour

- standards expected from staff and children in your setting
- how and with whom concerns can be raised
- create an ethos where staff feel they are listened to and taken seriously.

Personnel procedures

- disciplinary issues
- ongoing suitability issues
- 'whistle blowing'.

Supervision

 EYFS 3.19–EYFS 3.22

The importance of supervision is now formally recognised within the EYFS as a welfare requirement. Lord Laming identified, in his 2009 progress report 'The Protection of Children in England' that 'Staff supervision and the assurance of good practice must become elementary requirements in each service'. According to the report, 'Analysing child deaths and serious injury through abuse and neglect: what can we learn?' 'Supervision is also essential to help staff cope with the emotional demands of work with children and their families – and this has an impact at all levels of intervention, not just in social work'. Staff need to feel confident and competent in carrying out their roles responsibilities. Supervision is essential in promoting, developing and consolidating skills, judgement and confidence.

 Remember

The Plymouth serious case review (2010) into Little Teds Nursery highlights, 'supervision is important in assisting staff in coping with the emotional demands of the job, as well as enabling them to reflect on the meaning of their gut feelings'.

Supervision format

 EYFS 3.20

A supervisor needs to develop a professional, trusting relationship with staff in order to create an atmosphere that safeguards children first. Supervisors need to devise planned meetings ensuring the frequency is appropriate for the level of staff being supervised. According to the Ofsted evaluation schedule, high-quality professional supervision based on consistent and sharply focused evaluations of the impact of staff's practice. It is a contributory factor to outstanding leadership and management of the early years provision. Supervision sessions should have a very clear remit as an arena for:

- professional discussions
- seeking advice and expertise

- reflection
- 'whistle blowing'.

Do you operate a culture of honesty within your setting? A whistle blowing procedure can help to safeguard children from would-be perpetrators. However, staff need to feel able to share their concerns with senior management or outside the senior team, with trustees, governors or other authority figures if appropriate.

Remember

The Birmingham serious case review (2013) into Little Stars Nursery outlines, 'Effective supervision is important and this should support staff in reflecting on any concerns they may have about the behaviour of a colleague' (Wonnacott, J. Serious case review case No.2010–11/3. 2013).

Ensure lines of accountability are clear and transparent. Public Concern at Work is the 'whistle blowing' charity. See http://www.pcaw.org.uk/ for advice.

Remember

'Working Together to Safeguard Children' (DFE 2013) guidance states: 'There should be a guarantee that procedures can be invoked in ways that do not prejudice the whistle-blower's own position and prospects' (p294).

Managers and deputies

 EYFS 3.21 and CR 4.3

A manager's role is pivotal to the success of a setting and the well-being of children. Managers are accountable and need to take ownership of the day-to-day quality of practice, decision making and health and safety of all children and adults. An appointed deputy is also accountable and in the absence of the manager must be able to escalate concerns, diffuse situations and safeguard children at all times. Outlined below is the minimum qualification requirements highlighted in the EYFS for managers, deputies and the staff team.

Minimum qualification requirements are:

Manager

- Full and relevant level 3 qualification and two years' experience of working in an early years setting or other suitable experience.

Named deputy

- Full and relevant level 3 qualification, and deemed capable and qualified to take charge in the manager's absence.

Team

- At least half of the staff team must hold a full and relevant level 2 qualification.

Remember

If inspectors find there is ineffective monitoring of staff resulting in inconsistent practice and poor identification of training needs and staff do not have access to an adequate programme of professional development, this may contribute to an inspection judgement of 'inadequate' as it may impact on the quality of how well the early years provision meets the needs of the range of children who attend the setting.

Appraisals

 EYFS 3.22

One of the criteria inspectors consider when judging the leadership and management of the early years provision relates to how effective systems are for performance management and the continuous professional development of staff. Think about how well your staff, any trainees or students and apprentices are monitored, coached, mentored and supported, and how under-performance is tackled.

Remember

Point 5.73 of the serious case review into Little Teds Nursery in Plymouth (2010) highlighted the lack of supervision, combined with a lack of performance management, appraisal and a staff team who blurred the boundaries between their personal and professional lives, helped contribute to the perpetrators' power base within the setting.

Professional development

 EYFS 3.22

Your programme for ongoing staff professional development needs to arise from identified staff needs and form part of your self-evaluation systems in order to ensure all training requirements continue to be met.

Inspectors will be looking for evidence of:

- ongoing professional development
- the extent and range of completed training, including child protection
- the impact of that training in improving children's well-being.

Staff need opportunities to share their newly acquired knowledge and skills from training. Ensure you provide these for staff to undertake research tasks and activities in order to put theory into practice. This helps to demonstrate that training has an impact on your setting.

Remember

According to the Nutbrown Review (2012), 'Practitioners who undertake regular Continuing Professional Development (CPD) show a proper respect for the children and families they work with, taking a professional pride in their work, and demonstrating an understanding of their responsibility to constantly improve their practice and enhance the experience they are able to offer young children' (p52, 'Foundations For Quality. The independent review of early education and childcare qualifications. Final Report', June 2012).

First aid

 EYFS 3.24 and CR 1.3

There must be at least one person, qualified in paediatric first aid on the premises at all times and must accompany children on outings. Please see Chapter 9 for full information on first aid requirements.

Sufficient grasp of English

 EYFS 1.8 and EYFS 3.25

All staff must have a sufficient grasp of English to ensure the well-being of the children in their care. Staff need to be able to:

- summon emergency help where necessary
- liaise with other agencies in English
- keep the required records in English
- read and understand instructions in English, such as safety instructions, information on safety and administration of medicines or food hygiene and/or food allergies
- support children to develop their communication, language and literacy skills in English.

Staff need to consider how to include opportunities for children to use their home language in their play and learning, while ensuring children are developing a strong grasp of English.

Remember

The policy, 'Improving the quality and range of education and childcare from birth to 5 years' sets out what basic skills and knowledge are needed by people working with children, young people and families. It also outlines reforms to early years qualifications to make them more rigorous. For more information see 'Improving the quality and range of education and childcare from birth to 5 years' (DFE 2013). https://www.gov.uk/government/policies/improving-the-quality-and-range-of-education-and-childcare-from-birth-to-5-years.

Law

It is a legal requirement for those on the voluntary part of the Childcare Register to have at least one person who has had training either in the common core skills and knowledge or who holds a relevant level 2 qualification.

Supervision and appraisals are good opportunities to discuss any issues around staff literacy skills. Ensure that information going home with children, such as daily diaries and progress charts are well-written, free from spelling or grammar errors and legible.

Childminders

The above guidance applies to childminders who also need to consider:

 EYFS 3.23

Prospective childminders must complete EYFS training prior to registration being granted. As a childminder you are responsible for the children at all times as well as managing any assistants you may employ. This includes their CPD. Ensure you keep up to date with mandatory training, such as first aid.

Employers' responsibility

 HSWA 1974 Section 2(2)(c)

Employers have a legal duty to provide employees with information, instruction, training and supervision necessary to enable that person to understand the responsibilities of their role and enable them to do their job safely.

This provision runs through other health and safety regulations, such as the Management of Health and Safety at Work Regulations 1999 and is the cornerstone of an effective health and safety management system.

 The Management of Health and Safety at Work Regulations 1999 Regulation 13(1)

These regulations are more explicit and explain what is required and when. The employer is required to assess the capability of their employees in relation to health and safety and the tasks that are required.

Remember

Identify the training needs of the person in relation to the job responsibility and job role. You need to assess their competence and plan your training programme around this assessment.

 The Management of Health and Safety at Work Regulations 1999 Regulation 13(2)(a)

The regulations require an employer to provide health and safety training to their employees

- on recruitment – induction training and training specific to the job.

Regardless of any previous experience the employee must receive induction training. This training should cover emergency procedures, for example, evacuation and fire safety procedures, first aid and accident reporting specific to the employer's business.

Even if the new recruit has come from the same or a similar sector, it is highly unlikely that any two businesses are identical in terms of premises, management structure, procedures etc. Specific training in relation to the job should be provided.

Remember

Certain types of job may require specialist training. The Early Years Foundation Stage (EYFS) requires that those persons working in childcare hold certain qualifications.

→ The Management of Health and Safety at Work Regulations 1999 Regulation 13(2)(b)

The regulations require an employer to provide health and safety training to their employees:

- on being exposed to new or increased risks
- because of a change of job or responsibility
- because of the introduction of new or modified equipment
- because of the introduction of new technology
- because of a new system of work or a modification to an existing system of work.

An employee must receive information and training about any risks to their health and safety while at work and any controls or safety precautions in place to remove or reduce those risks.

Changes to the job, the environment, equipment or working procedures require a risk assessment review. If the risks change or increase then the employee must be advised. They must receive health and safety training in relation to any new or increased risks.

→ The Management of Health and Safety at Work Regulations 1999 Regulations 13(3)(a), 13(3)(b), 13(3)(c),

The training shall:

- be repeated periodically where appropriate – refresher training
- be reviewed and adapted to take account of changes and any new or increased risks
- be planned and should take place in working hours.

It is important to assess the outcome of any training to identify any gaps or further training needs. Refresher training may also be required to ensure skills are kept up to date, for example, first aiders. Refresher training also updates knowledge of procedures that are not be used everyday but are still important, for example, evacuation procedures.

Law

An employer cannot charge their employee for health and safety training.

Employee's responsibility

An employee has a duty under Section 7 of the Health and Safety at Work etc. Act 1974 to take reasonable care of his own health and safety and that of anyone else affected by his actions or omissions. There is also a duty to cooperate with the employer in health and safety matters.

 The Management of Health and Safety at Work Regulations 1999 Regulation 14(1)

The regulations require the employee to use work equipment provided by their employer in a correct manner and in accordance with the training and the information that they have received from their employer.

Types of training, assessment, review and records

Types of training are varied. Sometimes it is easy to assume that all training has to be provided by an external training provider and that it involves attending a formal course. This is not true. An employer must assess what is required in their business. Very often it may be a combination.

In-house training, for example:

- giving instruction on the evacuation procedure, showing where the first aid box is located, where the fire exits are located etc.
- on the job training, for example completed with another competent employee by coaching, shadowing, mentoring and supervising.

 Remember

Ensure that the employee assisting with the training is competent to undertake the task. This avoids new employees being trained to complete tasks in an unsuitable or unsafe method.

- Online training is popular as training can usually be completed in modules.
- External training courses, for example, specialist training through external training providers, first aid courses and NVQs.

Assessing training outcomes

Successful training can be assessed by talking to employees during and after completion of the training intervention. Also look at behaviour in the workplace and any improvements in the number of accidents/near misses and/or incidents.

Review training requirements

Assessing the outcomes will help to identify what went well as well as any further training needs or gaps. When planning training give priority to:

- new recruits
- young people
- positions that require specific training, for example, first aiders.

Training records

Employers should keep training records, including in-house training and any external training courses.

Maintaining records helps in planning training, for example, ensuring first aid refresher training takes place before certificates expire.

Remember

In the event of an accident or serious incident it can be very difficult to prove that training has been given in the absence of a signed training record or course certificate.

5 Management documentation

This chapter examines the myths around superfluous paperwork but reiterates the importance of what is essential. The effective administration of business is crucial to the quality of your setting, your success, reputation and compliance with legislation. The EYFS clearly outlines all required documentation to meet the safeguarding and welfare requirements. Other legislation must also be considered when implementing policies and procedures. Information is a precious asset and must be accurate, stored securely, processed efficiently and destroyed sensitively.

Health and safety is often blamed or cited as a reason for not doing something because there is too much paperwork. As part of the government's drive to reduce burdens on business and to promote better regulation, the Lofstedt Review was commissioned. The report entitled 'Reclaiming health and safety for all: An independent review of health and safety legislation' made a number of recommendations that have been welcomed by the government. This will result in certain changes to the law and some approved codes of practice and guidance. This is an ongoing process. To keep up to date with any changes, you can visit HSE's website and or sign up to e bulletins and podcasts at http://www.hse.gov.uk/news/subscribe/index.htm.

From researching and writing this book it is apparent that the requirements of the EYFS and health and safety law are not always consistent with each other. For example, the accident reporting requirements differ, resulting in a dual notification process. The requirements to record risk assessments differ, as in health and safety law there is mainly a two-tier approach, based on the number of employees in the business. This can lead to confusion amongst providers and inspectors.

The requirements for health and safety management documentation in this chapter precede those of the EYFS. However, the EYFS is a registration and a management assessment audit process. If a document is required under the EYFS but is not required under health and safety law, then the document still has to be in place for the provider to meet the requirements of the EYFS.

Maintaining records and sharing information

 EYFS 3.67–EYFS 3.70 and CR 8

It is vital that you have established protocols for sharing relevant information about children's well-being and progress, in addition to escalating concerns and eliciting support from other agencies.

Think about how you share information with:

- parents and carers
- other professionals
- social services
- police
- Ofsted.

To demonstrate that your setting is managed efficiently your records need to be:

- well-organised
- relevant to your setting
- reflect consideration of inclusion
- up to date
- made available to parents and carers
- reviewed and evaluated
- available for inspection.

Remember

It is good practice to give parents and carers the opportunity to formally comment on children's care, learning and any other issues. Do your records reflect evidence of this?

Providing information to parents and carers

 EYFS 2.2–2.3, EYFS 2.5, EYFS 3.72, CR 9.1, CR 9.2 and CR 9.3

Providers must maintain a two-way flow of information with parents and carers. It is important to consider if children attend more than one setting and how information can be gathered and exchanged.

Strategies for maintaining a two-way flow of information include:

- a daily diary that children take home and bring back to the setting
- using texts/emails
- photographs
- children's learning journeys
- collecting comprehensive information prior to children starting
- regular newsletters.

Remember

Ensure you have permission from parents and carers to use different strategies for sharing information. Be sensitive to, and make arrangements for, families who may have English as an additional language or literacy difficulties.

Access and confidentiality

 EYFS 3.67 and EYFS 3.68, CR 8

Confidentiality is about discretion and trust. As providers, you will hold sensitive information on children and their families that you must keep safe. It may not be feasible for you to keep documentation on site, for example, if you operate from a shared building with no secure storage facilities. In this instance you must inform Ofsted that you intend to store documents securely off site. You will still be expected to make documents available during an inspection.

All providers have a duty to keep information safe and secure. You may have a mixture of paper and electronic information that requires protecting. You need to consider arrangements for storing and discussing information at your setting.

Ask yourself some security questions about how and where you store information:

Paper

- Do you have lockable filing cabinets?
- Who has access to the keys?

Electronic

- Are computers secure and password protected? Is encryption required?
- Do staff use memory sticks and are these secure?

Verbal

- Is there a place where confidential discussions can take place?
- How do you manage gossip amongst staff or parents and carers?

Consider staff conduct. Do you have a policy about staff taking children's records home to update them? What potential security breaches would this practice pose?

Think about:

- the level of information contained in children's files, home details, photographs and personal information
- household members and other adults having access to this information
- information being photocopied, uploaded to websites, lost, misplaced or stolen
- if you have permission from parents and/or carers for their children's personal details to be taken off site.

To ensure confidentiality is maintained and information is handled appropriately you need to:

- evaluate security systems for storing data
- be clear about who in your setting is responsible for ensuring information security
- ensure you have appropriate technical security systems in place
- have robust policies and procedures
- recruit reliable, well-trained staff and use supervision appropriately
- be ready to respond to any information security breaches swiftly and effectively.

! Remember

The Children Act 1989 emphasis is to ensure that the welfare of the child is paramount. It is imperative that you have clear policies and procedures regarding when confidentiality must be superseded to escalate concerns. You must ensure documentation is made available to any professional who has a right to see them.

 Law

Be aware of your responsibilities under:

- The Childcare Act 2006
- The Childcare (Disqualification) Regulations 2009
- Working Together to Safeguard Children 2013
- Data Protection Act (DPA) 1998
- Freedom of Information Act 2000.

For more information on regulations see Appendix 2.

Arrangements for safeguarding children

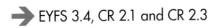 EYFS 3.4, CR 2.1 and CR 2.3

Staff need to be clear that they have a duty to escalate concerns and must:

- take all necessary steps to protect a child from harm or abuse
- report a suspected abuser(s)
- report a crime.

Privacy of children

 EYFS 3.69

All staff must ensure that children's privacy is respected. Ensure you have parental consents to gather data that may be used for statistical analysis. For example, data relating to ethnicity, disability, gender, religion and so on. Ensure you have parental permission to take photographs of children, especially if you plan to use images on websites or in publicity materials to promote your setting. Parents and carers have a right to see all records relating to their child provided no exemptions have been applied under the DPA.

 Law

Exemptions from the Data Protection Act (DPA) 1998 can be granted that can withhold certain information being released. For example, a psychologist may not grant permission for a full assessment to be shared with certain other parties. See http://www.ico.gov.uk for further advice on exemptions.

Retention of records

 EYFS 3.70, CR 7.3 and CR 8

The EYFS states that individual records must be retained for a reasonable period of time after children have left the premises.

Individual records may include:

- nappy change sheets
- feeding charts
- sleep records
- attendance registers
- children's information sheets
- medication records
- accident and incident records.

A 'reasonable period' is usually interpreted as a three year minimum or after the next inspection. However, you must check the liability sections of your insurance policy regarding records relating to accidents, safeguarding issues and medication as you may be required to keep these for a longer time period.

Information about the child

 EYFS 3.71 and CR 8

The EYFS outlines the minimum requirements you need to ascertain about a child including:

- child's full name, home address
- child's date of birth
- name and address of every parent and carer
- any other person who has parental responsibility for the child
- which parent(s) the child normally lives with
- emergency contact details for parents and carers
- a daily record of the names of children and their hours of attendance
- a record of any accidents to children occurring at the childcare setting
- any medicine administered, including the date and circumstances and parental consents
- details for all adults living or working on the premises.

 Remember

It is important you consider inclusion issues when gathering information to meet children's individual needs. Think about children's home language, cultural or religious needs, medical and dietary requirements and any special needs or special educational needs.

Information for parents and carers

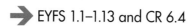 EYFS 1.1–1.13, EYFS 3.72, CR 9.1, CR 9.2 and CR 9.3

Provide information about how the EYFS is delivered in your setting. This might be through displays, leaflets, open learning sessions and training workshops. Include information about how parents and carers can obtain more information about the Early Years Foundation Stage in order to support their child's learning, including http://www.foundationyears.org.uk, a website developed by the government, professionals and the voluntary and community sector, to give advice from pregnancy to school age children.

Organisation and information about activities and routines

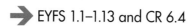 EYFS 1.1–1.13 and CR 6.4

Information relating the various activities and experiences provided for children in your setting and the daily routine should be outlined to parents and carers. This ensures children's families can contribute to the learning process and support their child's learning at home. It also offers parents and carers the opportunity to update staff on children's individual care needs and changes in routine.

Organisation and information about special educational needs or disabilities

 EYFS 2.2, YFS 3.66, CR 6.4 and CR 6.5

Children who have learning difficulties and disabilities need carefully targeted and tailored support. Parents and carers need to be reassured that their children will be welcomed and included in all aspects of your setting.

Ensure your policies and procedures reflect legislation including Special Educational Needs and Disability Act 2001 and Disability Discrimination Act 1995 and 2005.

Law

From 2014 parents and carers are to get a new legal right to buy in specialist SEN and disabled care for their children. Ensure your appointed SENCO keeps up to date with legislative changes.

Information about food and drinks provided for children

 EYFS 3.45, EYFS 3.46 and EYFS 3.47

Children may have many opportunities to enjoy a nutritious range of snacks, meals and drinks while at your setting. Children who stay all day will be provided with, breakfast, lunch, tea, snack and drinks. Parents and carers need to know what food and drinks children will be given. It is usual to display a menu prominently in order for parents and carers to see the variety of meals offered to children.

For babies and toddlers you may be required to complete food diaries so families can monitor children's reactions to new foods being introduced to their child's diet and ensure children are drinking enough fluids.

Children unable to leave the premises

 EYFS 3.61 and CR 5.2

You must have clear policies and procedures in the event of:

- parents and carers failing to collect a child
- a child going missing from your setting
- a child going missing while on a trip.

For uncollected children you need to consider:

- How often you update parent and carer contact details?
- Are staff expected to notify a manager of the situation?
- What is your interpretation of late – 15 minutes after closing?
- Are there two members of staff on duty at the end of the day?
- Who would try and contact the parent or carer and all emergency contact numbers for the child?
- If the emergency contact numbers for the child do not illicit a response, what next?

! Remember

Include timescales and relevant contact numbers in your policy for:

- social services team
- social services team; out of hours
- Ofsted
- police
- Local Authority Designated Officer (LADO).

For missing children you need to consider:

- Is your missing child procedure clear, effective and understood by all staff?
- Who will take the lead in your setting to liaise with police, Ofsted and staff?
- How will you deploy staff to ensure that remaining children stay calm and adequately supervised during a search?
- How are parents to be informed if their child is missing?
- Who is responsible for contacting the police and parents if the child is not found after searching the premises?
- What is the procedure and timescale for recording any incidents and informing the relevant agencies for example, Ofsted and the Children's Duty Team?

Complaints

 EYFS 3.73 and EYFS 3.74, CR 7.1–CR 7.6

Please refer to Chapter 1 and audit tools for information relating to dealing with complaints.

Records to be kept and information about the provider

 EYFS 3.75 and CR 8

The following information must be held by settings:

- name, address and telephone number of the providers and all others living on the premises or employed (this does not apply to childminders)
- name, address and telephone number of any other person who has unsupervised contact with children at the setting
- a daily record that reflects children's hours of attendance and their allocated key persons.

Ofsted registration certificate

➜ EYFS 3.75 and CR 15.1

A valid Ofsted registration certificate must be displayed within your setting.

Public liability insurance

➜ EYFS 3.62 and CR 14.2

A valid public liability certificate must be available for inspection and displayed at the setting. Public liability insurance is covered in more detail in Chapter 6.

Childminders

The above guidance applies to childminders who also need to consider:

➜ CR 9.1 and CR 9.3

Written statements relating to safeguarding and complaints must be available to parents and/or carers. Ensure you have details of Ofsted's address for parents and carers.

Health and safety

The following list details management documentation that may be required under health and safety law in certain circumstances.

Health and safety policy

Health and safety policies are discussed in Chapter 1.

Guidance and a template on a health and safety policy for small businesses are available at http://www.hse.gov.uk/contact/faqs/policy.htm.

Risk assessment

Risk assessment discussed in Chapter 7.

Example risk assessments, a template and the five steps guidance to risk assessment is available at http://www.hse.gov.uk/risk/fivesteps.htm.

Fire risk assessment and procedures for dealing with imminent danger

Fire risk assessment is discussed in Chapter 6.

In England and Wales, information about fire safety is at http://www.communities.gov.uk/fire/firesafety/firesafetylaw/. This includes guidance on how to complete your assessment. In Scotland you can obtain information at http://www.scotland.gov.uk.

You also need to plan for an emergency. The responsible person/ employer is required to implement evacuation procedures to be followed in the event of:

- a serious or imminent danger
- a fire
- a gas leak
- bomb threat or an explosion.

The Control of Substances Hazardous to Health Regulations 2002 (as amended) (COSHH)

COSHH is discussed in Chapter 6.

Guidance on the regulations, how to comply and examples of COSHH assessments are available at http://www.hse.gov.uk/coshh/.

The Manual Handling Operations Regulations 1992 (as amended)

Guidance on manual handling and tools called manual handling assessment charts (MAC) to help with assessments are available at http://www.hse.gov.uk/contact/faqs/manualhandling.htm.

The Personal Protective Equipment at Work Regulations 1992 (as amended) (PPE)

PPE is discussed in Chapter 6.

'A short guide to the Personal Protective Equipment at Work Regulations 1992' is available at http://www.hse.gov.uk/pubns/indg174.pdf.

The Provision and Use of Work Equipment Regulations 1998 (PUWER)

Work equipment is discussed in Chapter 6.

Guidance on the regulations called 'Simple guide to the Provision and Use of Work Equipment Regulations 1998' is available at http://www.hse.gov.uk/pubns/indg291.pdf.

The Health and Safety (Display Screen Equipment) Regulations 1992 (DSE)

Guidance on these regulations is available at http://www.hse.gov.uk/msd/dse/.

The Control of Asbestos Regulations 2012

In April 2012, new regulations were introduced to consolidate the law on asbestos and the management of asbestos containing material (ACMs) in non-domestic premises. The law requires the duty holder to manage asbestos in the premises. More information about these regulations is at http://www.hse.gov.uk/asbestos/regulations.htm.

A leaflet called 'Managing asbestos in buildings: A brief guide' is available at http://www.hse.gov.uk/pubns/indg223.pdf.

Legionella

A combination of the Management of Health and Safety at Work Regulations 1999 and the Control of Substances Hazardous to Health Regulations 2002 (as amended) require a suitable and sufficient assessment to identify and assess the risk of exposure to legionella from the work activities and the water systems to be undertaken. The assessment must also identify precautionary measures to be taken. More information about the control of legionella is available at http://www.hse.gov.uk/legionnaires/index.htm.

A leaflet called 'Legionnaires' disease: A brief guide for duty holders', is available at http://www.hse.gov.uk/pubns/indg458.pdf.

Law

The requirement to record significant findings from assessments is not always consistent and what is required can vary in different regulations. You need to check the individual pieces of law, using the guidance on HSE's website.

Accidents, ill health and dangerous occurrences

Accidents are discussed in Chapter 8. The records that you need to consider are:

- accident book/form
- reportable accidents records, 'over three day' injury records, dangerous occurrences and occupational diseases records
- first aid treatment records.

Electricity

Electricity is discussed in Chapter 6.

Records should be kept of any formal inspection and testing of the electrical system.

There is a prescribed report for inspection and testing to determine the condition of the electrical installation. This is known as the 'electrical installation condition report' and replaces the previous 'periodic inspection' form.

Certificates are also prescribed for completion and minor works to the electrical system.

The 'competent person' completing the work provides these. They should be completed in full and signed.

Although the law does not require records to be kept of portable appliance inspection or testing or the labelling of equipment, it is good practice to do so.

Gas appliances

Gas is discussed in Chapter 6.

Employers and self-employed people must ensure that any gas appliance, flue or installation pipework installed at a place of work under their control, is installed and maintained in a safe condition.

A 'competent person' should install, inspect, maintain and carry out any work on gas appliances pipework and flues. The Gas Safe Register recommends that this inspection take place at least once a year. The 'competent person' is an engineer who is registered on the Gas Safe Register and this person should provide you with certification.

Maintenance records

Certain types of equipment may require examination and inspection through legislation, for example:

- the inspection and testing of lifting equipment including passenger and goods lifts.

Maintenance may be detailed in standards, for example:

- the inspection and testing of fire detection fire alarm and emergency lighting; the inspection and maintenance of play equipment.

The manufacturer, supplier or installer of a piece of equipment may recommend maintenance.

It is good practice to keep a maintenance log on equipment where failure could lead to an unsafe condition.

Monitoring records

The risk-based regulations require an employer or responsible person to ensure that control measures are effective. Monitoring can be undertaken by auditing procedures, working practices and the working environment.

Information, instruction, training and supervision

Training is discussed in Chapter 4.

Providing information, instruction and training is a key theme throughout health and safety law.

Yet in many of the regulations highlighted, there is no legal requirement to keep training records. Without proper records it is very difficult to demonstrate that you have fulfilled your legal obligations, or to prove that certain persons whom you appoint to complete tasks are competent.

Insurance

An employer is required by law to have current employers' liability insurance to cover the cost of any claims for compensation that an injured employee might make.

Guidance on employers' liability insurance can be found at HSE's website at http://www.hse.gov.uk/pubns/hse40.pdf.

Staff consultation

Staff consultation is discussed in Chapter 1.

Under Health and Safety (Information for Employees) Regulations 1989 (as amended) you have to provide information to employees. You can comply by displaying the 'Health and Safety Law Poster' or providing the equivalent pocket card or leaflet.

Management documentation of food safety

Food safety is discussed in Chapter 11.

The following list details management documentation that may be required under food safety law:

- registration of food premises
- food safety management system and records, for example temperature control, pest control records and proof of purchase from food suppliers
- training records for staff and the person responsible for implementing and monitoring the management system.

Law

Due to the Lofstedt Review there are changes taking place in health and safety law and guidance. The aim of these changes is to simplify requirements and to reduce the burden on business. HSE is reviewing a number of their approved codes of practice (ACOPs). These documents may be withdrawn, replaced or amended. The aim is to make them simpler to use. You can get up-to-date information about these changes at http://www.hse.gov.uk/consult/condocs/cd241.htm.

6 Safe and suitable environment

The EYFS outlines the importance of play and children being cared for within a safe, suitable and secure environment. Childcare can be provided in a variety of settings, including a family home, village hall, purpose built premises or on a vehicle such as a 'play bus'. Each type of setting presents its own set of security and safety challenges. Staff are responsible in ensuring toys and equipment are of high quality, and are safe and suitable for all children.

There is a general duty under the Health and Safety at Work etc. Act 1974 to ensure that a workplace is safe, including access and egress. It also covers welfare requirements, such as temperature and toilet facilities for staff. The Workplace (Health Safety and Welfare) Regulations 1992 provide detailed requirements for safe workplaces for workers.

This chapter provides a summary of the legal requirements to provide and maintain a safe and suitable environment and signposts to further, detailed guidance in specific areas. It highlights some of the issues relating to structure and equipment and practice that have caused serious accidents and fatalities in settings.

Premises

 EYFS 3.53

The Ofsted registration and suitability handbook defines premises as any area or vehicle. You may have sole use of premises or share premises with other groups and service users. During a registration visit or at inspection you need to:

- identify any risks associated with your premises and equipment
- explain what you do to reduce or eliminate risks.

 CR 5.1

The registered person must ensure that the premises and equipment used for the purposes of the childcare are safe and suitable for that childcare. You must also assess the risks associated with others areas of the premises or risks posed by other service users.

You need to consider the following :

- Sufficient space for each child and organisation of space.
- Heat, light, ventilation, state of repair and cleanliness.
- Access to an outdoor play area and the proximity to your setting.
- Suitable and sufficient food preparation areas, nappy changing, toilets, sleep areas, play areas.
- Fire safety arrangements.
- Arrangements for the safety of children if you share premises.

Law

Do you need planning permission for your premises? You need to ensure that your premises comply with planning and building control regulations.

Remember

Inspectors will want to be reassured that children can play and learn in a safe and suitable environment. Ineffectual checking systems and a poor attitude to safety can be linked to leadership and management of your setting, and may reflect badly on your inspection outcome.

Premises, fit for purpose; equal opportunities and inclusion

 EYFS 3.66, CR 6.4 and CR 6.5

Think about the equipment, age of children and their individual needs in particular rooms. While it is good practice to ensure rooms are welcoming, you must prioritise safety. Ensure you have evidence that rooms used by children are safe and staff are alert to changes posed by children's inquisitiveness, increasing mobility and specific needs.

 Law

It is your responsibility to ensure you have up-to-date information on environmental health requirements, fire safety and legislation and that you meet these requirements.

Remember

Keep up to date with product recalls as even reputable toys and equipment can develop unanticipated faults. You can check for product recalls on http://www.tradingstandards.gov.uk/advice/advice-recall-list.cfm.

 EYFS 3.1 and EYFS 3.53

Ensure you can provide a stimulating environment for all children in your care. A wide selection of good quality, sustainable, suitable toys, equipment and resources is essential. Look for safety symbols when buying toys and resources.

Remember

Safety symbols alone are not a guarantee of safety or quality, but a guide to help with decision making when choosing toys and resources. For more information on toy safety see http://www.rospa.com/homesafety/adviceandinformation/product/toy-safety.aspx.

Security of premises

 EYFS 3.61, CR 5.2, CR 5.3 and CR 5.4

The registered person must ensure that a child is unable to leave the premises without permission. Your premises must be secure. Ensure you have robust systems in place for children to arrive safely, not leave the premises without permission and restrict unauthorised adults gaining access. An up-to-date record of children's hours of attendance is essential. An exception to this would be where the childcare is open access childcare, or where the child is aged eight or over and the parent of the child has agreed that they may leave the provision unaccompanied.

Think about all aspects of the outdoor area also when considering children's safety.

- Car park hazards – have an arrival and departure policy to minimise risks to children from cars parking, reversing and driving in the vicinity of children.
- Security of the outdoor area – can children escape easily, can strangers gain access easily?
- Check to see if children can climb over, under or through fencing or open gates or bolts.
- Check if unknown adults could access the area. Think about how staff would challenge an unknown adult.
- Be aware of the local area and how children could access the road or water hazards such as ponds off-site.

Think about the surrounding area of your setting and the human element of risk management.

Are you satisfied absolutely that:

- all play areas are secure, adults are vigilant and children are learning to take responsibility for their own safety?
- you are aware of hazards in the vicinity of your setting?

Think about the worst case scenario. If a child escaped from your setting, what would be the risks?

- Are you satisfied that you have effective control measures in place?
- Do you need to review your risk assessment now to reflect your findings?

Cleanliness and hygiene

 EYFS 3.1, EYFS 3.53 and CR 5.1

Implement regular, consistent cleaning and hygiene routines in addition to encouraging hand washing. Make staff aware of their responsibilities to keep areas and equipment in a safe, suitable condition.

Cross-infection risks must be minimised and the following items need to be regularly, cleaned, washed and disinfected:

- toys, especially baby toys that children put in their mouths
- highchairs and straps
- cuddly toys, dolls and dolls' clothes
- dressing-up clothes and hats
- children's tables and chairs
- work surfaces
- feeding utensils including, bottles, bowls and cutlery

- children's bedding
- potties and toilet seats.

Remember

Soiled items, such as tissues, wipes and nappies all contain germs. Think about how staff and children dispose of waste. Do they have access to a bin? Does the bin have a lid?

Health and safety policy

 EYFS 3.1, EYFS 3.53 and CR 5.1

The EYFS outlines that providers are required to implement health and safety policies. See health and safety section of this chapter.

Do you actively involve all service users including families by providing training workshops on safety and accident prevention information?

Law

You must have regard for other legislation. Please refer to the other half of this chapter for specific legislative information on health and safety.

Remember

Consider everyone at risk or specialist events when devising your policies. For example:

- staff working in isolation
- lone workers
- fundraising events.

Emergency evacuation

 EYFS 3.54

As a registered provider you must demonstrate that you have reviewed and assessed fire safety arrangements. This includes having procedures and equipment in place that can be utilised in the event of an emergency. Your purpose in an evacuation is to ensure everyone leaves the building swiftly, calmly and safely. Ensure you have an up-to-date list of everyone in the building. See fire safety law within this chapter.

It is imperative that all fire detection equipment is in working order. This includes smoke detectors, correctly installed with functioning batteries.

Ensure fire exits and doors are accessible at all times of the day, free from obstructions and can be opened easily in the event of an emergency. At the beginning and end of sessions be alert to parents and carers obstructing exits with pushchairs, prams or bags. Ofsted have protocols for liaising with the fire service and recommend that providers seek advice from their local fire safety officer when devising policies and procedures for fire safety and evacuation.

Smoking

 EYFS 3.55 and CR 1.8

There must be a no-smoking policy in place and no-smoking notices displayed throughout the building. A larger setting may have an allocated area for smoking. This must be away from children and not an area about to be used by children. It must comply with smoke-free legislation.

Organisation

 EYFS 1.11–1.4, EYFS 3.56 and CR 6.1–CR 6.5

Organise the space in your setting to ensure each age group can enjoy a full learning experience. Think about how you deploy staff, equipment and resources. Most settings plan rooms to cater for babies, toddlers, pre-school and school aged children. Mixed age groups of children can pose difficulties as they each pursue their own interests, at their own pace. Have a flexible approach and ensure all staff supervise children effectively in order to avoid accidents. Think about the age and mobility of children. Consider if young babies and crawling and fully mobile children pose a hazard to each other.

Each room needs to have sufficient toys, resources and storage facilities. Plan to cater for children's basic needs including mealtimes, sleeps and outdoor play. Ensure that space standards are adhered to:

- Children under two years: 3.5 m² per child.
- Two year olds: 2.5 m² per child.
- Children aged three to five years: 2.3 m² per child.

This needs to be clear, useable space suitable for use by children and cannot include storage areas, staff areas, cloakrooms, utility rooms, kitchens and toilets.

Suitable for children with disabilities

 EYFS 3.57, EYFS 3.66, CR 6.4 and CR 6.5

When working with children with disabilities, it is important to help children in overcoming potential barriers to their learning. Think about individual children in your setting. Do they need support with mobility and coordination? Do they need visual or hearing support? Review and evaluate your environment and resources making reasonable adjustments.

You can:

- provide resources at children's level, such as placing sand and water troughs on the floor or on a low table
- adapting resources, such as dressing-up clothes with easy fastenings so all children can engage in imaginative play
- focus on lighting, colour and textures for children with visual needs.

 Law

The Equality Act 2010 (Disability) Regulations 2010, part 4 outlines; Reasonable Adjustments to Physical Features. This gives disabled people important rights of access to everyday services. Service providers have an obligation to make reasonable adjustments to premises or to the way they provide a service.

Outdoor access and activities

 EYFS 3.53 and EYFS 3.57

Children must have opportunities for outdoor activities on a daily basis. Children benefit from fresh air and exercise and most activities undertaken indoors can be successfully implemented outside.

Think about your outdoor area.

- Can children access it easily?
- Is it secure, safe and risk assessed?
- Does it offer a variety of play experiences, such as relaxation area, climbing, exploration area and growing areas?
- Does it offer a variety of resources, den building, mark making, balance and cycling opportunities, books, small world toys, role play equipment and climbing apparatus?

Accidents in playgrounds can be attributed to problems with equipment, individuals or a combination of both. Out of doors things can be thrown over a fence into the area where children play so check the area for broken glass, needles, cigarette ends and animal excrement on a regular basis.

Remember

Reflect seasonal changes, such as when berries and brambles are growing in your risk assessment of the outdoors.

Ensure staff are aware of the following points when caring for children outdoors.

- Staff must ensure children are supervised outdoors, especially while using outdoor play equipment.
- Children need to wear suitable clothes especially footwear, when using outdoor equipment and climbing.
- Sometimes the weather dictates that it is not safe for children to use outdoor equipment because of slip hazards.
- Children need to know how to use equipment and what behaviour is not acceptable while using equipment.

Equipment issues that can lead to accidents include:

- poor design and failure to comply to safety standards
- incorrect and unsafe installation
- unsuitable and unsafe surface underneath equipment
- unsuitable for the age group of children
- making adaptations to equipment, such as tying on ribbons or ropes
- inadequate maintenance of equipment and surrounding areas.

Consider the usage of equipment and purchase good quality equipment that meets safety standards that can endure heavy duty use. Only use equipment according to manufacturer's instructions, e.g.

resist the temptation to add on accessories. Make sure equipment has been installed correctly and is fixed in position.

Remember

Retain evidence and documentation that equipment was installed correctly and is regularly maintained as this evidence may be requested in the event of an accident.

Think about the surface underneath – is it suitable, free from hazards and impact absorbing? For example, if you use bark, is it deep enough and free from animal excrement?

For more information see 'Accidents on Children's Playgrounds' http://www.rospa.com/leisuresafety/adviceandinformation/ playsafety/accidents-childrens-playgrounds.aspx.

Sleep and rest

 EYFS 3.58

It is important to adhere to, and respect, children's sleep routines. Some children need a comfort toy or blanket in order feel secure. Others need to hear music or a story before they can relax.

Ensure each child has their own individual bedding and, depending on the temperature of the room and thickness of the blanket, you might want to remove top layers of children's clothes. Always remove children's shoes before laying them down to sleep.

Some children resist having an afternoon nap. Be flexible and cater for any children who are not going to rest. Have a time limit as to how long staff should try to settle a child.

Be alert to any hazards within the vicinity of a cot or mattress. Ensure there is sufficient staff on duty to settle and monitor sleeping children. Comply with the checking timescales of your sleep policy and these checks need to be documented. There may always a chance to resuscitate a child successfully should they become unconscious, if they are found quickly and medical help can be sought promptly. See http://www.nhs.uk/Livewell/Childrenssleep/Pages/babysleeptips.aspx for more information on children's sleep.

Separate baby room for under 2s

 EYFS 3.58

The EYFS stipulates that children under two should have a separate baby room. This is in order for babies to be cared for in a homely environment. Careful planning of play opportunities may include resources to support a multi-sensory experience for children including soft music, different textures, smells and natural materials.

Transition

 EYFS 1.9, 2.6 and 3.58

Children are usually moved up to the next room depending on their age and stage of development. Once babies start walking confidently it is usual to plan their phased transition to the next room with visits in order for children to become familiar and develop self-confidence for the next phase of their development. It is also important to show how children are supported in moving onto the next stage of their education, such as going to nursery or school.

Toilets and hand basins

➡ EYFS 3.59

The EYFS outlines the ratio guidelines for toilets and wash-hand basins as being one for every ten children over the age of two. Adults should have access to separate toilet facilities. There needs to be a suitable, hygienic nappy changing area for babies. Having a supply of spare clothes and bedding is essential for babies and toddlers in order to ensure children are clean and comfortable. Staff need to adhere to your setting's hygiene policy for changing nappies. Intimate care needs to be conducted in line with your setting's safeguarding and inclusion policies. Encourage staff to:

- wear disposable gloves and aprons (just wearing one glove is not good practice)
- ensure the changing surface is cleaned after every use
- use wipes and creams as requested by parents and carers
- use spare clothes for children who have soiled clothes
- dispose of nappies hygienically.

Security systems

➡ EYFS 3.61 and CR 5.2–CR 5.5

Think about how you manage children's arrivals and departures in your setting.

- Do parents and carers sign their children in?
- Do staff 'meet and greet' families at arrival and departure times, checking doors are locked when parents and carers leave the building?
- Do you audit the registers throughout the day to ensure it is an accurate reflection of who is in the building?
- Do you ensure that children are only handed over to authorised adults?

Think about how you manage visitors to your setting.

- Do all staff know to check visitors' identification?
- Do visitors sign in?
- Are visitors identifiable and escorted while in your premises?

Insurance

 EYFS 3.62 and CR 14.2

Every setting must have valid public liability insurance in place. Your insurance certificate should be displayed and you need to check the date of expiry to ensure a renewed certificate is issued. You must inform your insurance company of any situation that is likely to result in a claim, such as if a child sustains a serious accident while at your setting. Be very careful not to invalidate your insurance.

Childminders

The above guidance applies to childminders who also need to consider the following

- Do you need planning permission to use your home for business?
- Where do you store alcohol? How will you prevent children from accessing it?
- How will you make all medication inaccessible to children?
- How will you maintain a smoke-free environment in your home?

 Remember

Childminders do not need to provide a separate baby room or provide separate toilet facilities for adults.

Safe and healthy environment

 HSWA 1974 Section 2(1)

The Act contains general requirements for a workplace. An employer has a duty to ensure so far as is reasonably practicable the health safety and welfare of their employees while at work. This general duty is further explained in Section 2(2) and in relation to the workplace.

 HSWA 1974 Sections 2(2)(d) and 2(2)(e)

An employer has a duty, so far is reasonably practicable to:

- maintain a safe place to work including access and egress to it
- provide and maintain a safe and healthy working environment with adequate welfare facilities.

 HSWA 1974 Section 4

There are also duties on people who are in control of premises and provide non-domestic premises as a place of work, for example, landlords. They have a duty to the people who are not their employees but who use the premises as a workplace.

The Workplace (Health, Safety and Welfare) Regulations 1992

These regulations set out minimum requirements for workplaces. An employer has a duty to ensure that the workplace complies with the regulations and duties are also placed on people in control of premises, such as landlords.

In general terms the regulations cover:

- maintenance of workplace, and of equipment, devices and systems
- ventilation
- temperature of indoor workplaces
- lighting
- cleanliness and waste materials
- room dimensions and space
- workstations and seating
- condition of floors and traffic routes
- windows, and transparent or translucent doors, gates and walls or gates
- windows, skylights and ventilators
- ability to clean windows etc. safely
- organisation of traffic routes
- doors and gates
- escalators and moving walkways
- sanitary conveniences for employees
- washing facilities
- drinking water
- accommodation for clothing
- facilities for changing clothing
- facilities for rest and to eat meals.

There is an approved code of practice entitled 'Workplace health, safety and welfare'. Workplace (Health, Safety and Welfare) Regulations 1992. Approved Code of Practice. This is available at http://www.hse.gov.uk/pubns/books/l24.htm.

A leaflet called 'Workplace health, safety and welfare. A short guide for managers' is available at http://www.hse.gov.uk/pubns/indg244.pdf.

Childminders

The Workplace (Health, Safety and Welfare) Regulations 1992 do not apply to domestic premises but remember you still have responsibilities under Section 3(2) of the main act.

A closer look at some of the workplace requirements

- **Temperature of indoor workplaces**
  During working hours the temperature in workrooms should be reasonable. In a childcare setting the temperature should be at least 16°C. A thermometer should be provided to enable the workplace temperature to be measured.

- **Windows, and transparent or translucent doors, gates and walls or gates**
  The approved code of practice gives examples of where safety materials or protection needs to be applied, defines safety materials and discusses alternative means of protection.

- **Sanitary conveniences for employees**
  A suitable and sufficient number of toilets need to be provided and maintained in a clean condition. No room containing a toilet should open directly into a room where food is processed, prepared or eaten or into a workroom.

  The rooms containing sanitary accommodation and washing facilities must be properly lit, ventilated and kept clean.

- **Washing facilities**
  Suitable and sufficient washing facilities need to be provided in the vicinity of toilets and accessible. This relates to the provision of wash hand-basins, which must be kept clean and provided with a supply of clean hot and cold water, or warm water, soap or another suitable means of cleaning and a means of hand drying.

  Although the law is not specific about what type of soap and hand drying facilities to use, liquid soap is recommended. You may wish to provide an antibacterial liquid soap.

  Disposable paper towels are recommended for hand drying.

  Bars of soap, fabric towels and nailbrushes at wash hand-basins can all provide a source of bacteria and spread infection. Warm air hand dryers may be provided but it is important that they are used to dry hands properly.

  The approved code of practice gives guidance on the ratios of toilets and washing facilities to be provided.

- **Smoking**
  Legislation is now in force across the United Kingdom that bans smoking in virtually all enclosed public places and workplaces and work vehicles.

Some specific workplace hazards to consider

Within the workplace, there may be structures, facilities and equipment that pose a specific hazard to children, unless proper controls are in place. The following hazards, along with any others specific to the individual setting require consideration under risk assessments. Many of the investigations into fatal and serious accidents at settings, have implicated a lack of risk assessment as a causative factor.

The list below is based on real accidents.

- **Blind/curtain cords and draw strings**
  These pose a potential trip hazard if trailing on the floor, these items can present a risk of entanglement and strangulation if accessible to children.

- **Doors**
  A number of accidents have occurred where children have trapped their fingers in doors and sustained a serious injury. Devices are available that can be fitted to doors to prevent finger entrapment.

- **Equipment**
  It is important to consider equipment that may be brought into the premises for use with the children in your care.

  Persons who design, manufacture, import or supply articles (equipment) for use at work also have responsibilities under Section 6 of the Health and Safety at Work etc. Act 1974. There are also requirements under consumer safety laws.

  You also have a responsibility to select safe and suitable equipment, assemble and use it correctly in accordance with manufacturer's instructions. You must ensure that it is suitable for purpose and maintained in a safe condition.

- **Falls from a height**
  Accidents have occurred when children have fallen from a height, for example, from a nappy changing bench. If such facilities are used, consider in your risk assessment how you will control this hazard. Falls from height can also occur on play equipment.

- **Food items and craft items**
  It is important to ensure that food given to a child is suitable for them to consume and does not present a choking hazard.

  Similar consideration should be given to craft activities where there is the potential for children to place items in their mouths and pose a choking hazard.

  Supervision also plays an important part in controlling these risks.

- **Grounds and gardens**
  Many issues need to be considered in this category. Site security is very important. Incidents have occurred where children have wandered from childcare sites. Other hazards may exist, such as poisonous and prickly plants, uneven paved surfaces and access to the road and traffic.

- **Organisation etc. of traffic routes**
  The movement of pedestrians and vehicles must be considered as part of the risk assessment programme. It is important to consider the safety of your children, visitors and contractors. Children in particular may not recognise danger or respond to warnings.

- **Radiators and hot pipes and surfaces**
  Hot surfaces, such as radiators, associated pipework can also pose a hazard and present a risk of burns and have caused injuries through contact.

- **Sleeping**
  Issues also exist surrounding the supervision and monitoring of babies and young children while sleeping. A robust and effective system based on risk assessment is required for the supervision and effective checking and monitoring of sleeping children.

- **Sources of heat hot water and heating**
  When considering risks of burns and scalds, do not forget to consider sources of heat, such as hot water temperature as well as heating equipment.
- **Stairs**
  Consider the children in your care and ensure that you provide a suitable infill or balusters on the stairs, preventing a child from falling through gaps or trapping body parts. Stair gates, where provided, need to be secured in place and constructed so as not to provide trapping points.

  Also consider other areas where stairs may be present, such as cellar access. Keep doors to these areas locked to prevent access by children, visitors or unauthorised people. Accidents have occurred where children and adults have fallen down cellar stairs/steps by opening the door and stepping through. Also consider any fire escapes.
- **Windows, skylights and ventilators**
  Windows, skylights and ventilators should be operated safely and without risk of a person falling through or out of the window. Where there is a risk of falling from a height, the opening of the window should be limited by a restrictor device to prevent the window from opening too far. There have been accidents where children have fallen out of windows.
- **Play equipment**
  There are recognised standards for external and internal play equipment. Play equipment and how you manage play on the equipment, for example, through controlling age, numbers and supervision needs to be considered through risk assessment.

  The Royal Society for the Prevention of Accidents (ROSPA) provides a number of information sheets on play equipment, on standards and inspection and maintenance regimes at http://www.rospa.com/leisuresafety/playsafety/.

  It is important to keep your records available. You may be required to produce them during an enforcement visit or as part of an accident investigation.

  You must never carry out alterations to play equipment without liaising with the provider/supplier. Any works should be documented and completed by a competent person.

Maintaining a safe environment

In any workplace things can change rapidly. The key principles for maintaining a safe environment are:

- planning setting objectives and prioritising through risk assessment
- assigning clear roles and responsibilities to staff
- implementing controls through procedures, reporting structures, management and action plans
- monitoring and review through planned health and safety audits and performance assessment
- informing and consulting with staff through staff meetings, safety representatives and safety committees.

Fire safety law

A review of fire safety laws has resulted in the Regulatory Reform (Fire Safety) Order 2005 that sets out the legal requirements for England and Wales. In Scotland, there are different regulations but the principal requirement is based on the concept of a fire risk assessment. This is the same in England and Wales.

The law places duties on the responsible person to take general fire precautions to:

- ensure, so far as is reasonably practicable, the safety of employees
- in the case of non-employees to take such general fire precautions as may be reasonable to ensure the premises are safe.

The requirements of Regulatory Reform (Fire Safety) Order 2005 mirror those of the Management of Health and Safety at Work Regulations 1999 and require the responsible person to:

- appoint 'competent person(s)'
- carry out fire risk assessment
- formulate an emergency plan
- consult and appoint staff to assist in fire safety arrangements
- provide non-employees with information about fire safety risks and arrangements
- cooperate and coordinate if you share a building
- provide information, instruction and training to employees
- maintain and ensure fire prevention and protection systems are working
- ensure that fire systems are maintained by a competent person where necessary.

In England and Wales, information about fire safety is available at http://www.communities.gov.uk/fire/firesafety/firesafetylaw/. This includes guidance on how to complete your assessment. In Scotland you can obtain information at http://www.scotland.gov.uk.

Electrical safety

→ The Electricity at Work Regulations 1989 Regulation 4

The Electricity at Work Regulations 1989 requires electrical systems to be constructed and maintained in order to prevent danger, so far as is reasonably practicable. For the purposes of the regulations, danger means a risk of injury.

A leaflet called 'Electrical safety and you. A brief guide' is available at http://www.hse.gov.uk/pubns/indg231.pdf. This provides information on how to comply with the regulations.

Portable appliance testing (PAT)

A guidance leaflet entitled 'Maintaining portable electric equipment in low-risk environments' is available and provides useful information about the inspection and maintenance of portable appliances; http://www.hse.gov.uk/pubns/indg236.pdf.

Gas safety

→ The Gas Safety (Installation and Use) Regulations 1998

Gas presents a hazard in the workplace which, if not properly controlled, can have fatal and catastrophic consequences. Badly installed and badly maintained equipment and fittings can present risk of fire and explosion or can emit toxic fumes, such as carbon monoxide.

Employers and self-employed people need to ensure that any gas appliance, flue or installation pipework, installed at a place of work under their control, is maintained in a safe condition.

Employers and self-employed people should take reasonable steps to ensure people undertaking work are competent, that is registered on the Gas Safe Register.

There is useful information on gas safety at http://www.hse.gov.uk/gas/domestic/index.htm.

The Provision and Use of Work Equipment Regulations 1998 (PUWER)

These regulations require that work equipment provided is constructed or adapted so that it is suitable for the intended use. There are also requirements to inspect and maintain work equipment.

Guidance on the regulations called 'Simple guide to the Provision and Use of Work Equipment Regulations 1998' is available at http://www.hse.gov.uk/pubns/indg291.pdf.

The Control of Substances Hazardous to Health Regulations 2002 (as amended) (COSHH)

These regulations require an employer to prevent or to control the exposure of their employees to hazardous substances in the workplace. This duty is also extended to other people whether or not they are at work, but where they are affected by the work activity. This is qualified by the term 'so far as is reasonably practicable'.

Hazardous substances may be chemicals, dusts, fumes and even bacteria and viruses.

In the childcare environment you need to consider substances, such as the chemicals that you use for cleaning, laundry, dishwashing and also processes such as:

- nappy changing
- assisted toileting
- laundering soiled linen
- dealing with body fluids, such as blood, vomit, faeces and urine.

You require strict infection control procedures, detailed in your hygiene policy to deal with these tasks.

The regulations require a suitable and sufficient assessment of the risk. This risk assessment is often referred to as a COSHH assessment(s) but it follows the same principles as the general risk assessments required under the Management of Health and Safety at Work Regulations 1999.

Guidance on the regulations, how to comply and examples of COSHH assessments are available at http://www.hse.gov.uk/coshh/.

The Personal Protective Equipment at Work Regulations 1992 (as amended) (PPE)

The use of personal protective equipment (PPE) as a control measure is always the last resort in the risk management hierarchy of controls. There are regulations covering the selection, use and maintenance of this type of equipment. Any PPE provided must be suitable for the intended risk and selected using assessment prior to selection and use.

Disposable aprons and gloves used for nappy changing would be classed as PPE.

'A short guide to the Personal Protective Equipment at Work Regulations 1992' is available at http://www.hse.gov.uk/pubns/indg174.pdf.

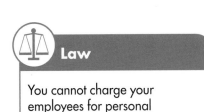

Law

You cannot charge your employees for personal protective equipment.

7 Risk assessment

The EYFS outlines the importance of ensuring children's safety with a 'common sense approach' to risk assessment. This includes ensuring risk assessments are reviewed and reflect any significant changes. The duty to ensure children's safety involves having regard for other legislation. The Management of Health and Safety at Work Regulations, 1999 must be adhered to in addition to the EYFS welfare requirements to ensure you comply with the law.

Many people remain confused about the concept of risk assessment and its application to business. Investigations into serious accidents and fatalities in the childcare sector have highlighted failings in risk assessment, often due to a lack of understanding of what is required. The media reporting of health and safety myths has not helped this situation. A notion has developed that people must be closeted against all risk. HSE has been active with their campaigns 'Myth of the month' and 'Myth busting challenge' to dispel these health and safety fables. Often such myths concentrate on insignificant imaginary risks, trivialise health and safety and detract from what is important.

The guidance provided by HSE stresses the importance of focusing on real risks in the workplace. It also recognises the importance of keeping things simple so that they are understood and used in practice. The emphasis is not on superfluous paperwork but on practical steps to be taken in completing a risk assessment, recording where necessary, significant findings and putting sensible precautions in place. The risk assessments and precautions need to be proportionate to the business.

This chapter will explain where the requirement to undertake risk assessment comes from. It will illustrate how to undertake a risk assessment and highlight the importance of risk assessment in accident prevention and the safe operation of a business. It also explores the human element, behaviour and impact on risk assessment in practice. Information relating to risk assessments for outings is covered in a separate chapter.

Policies, procedures and suitability of premises and equipment

→ EYFS 3.53, EYFS 3.61, EYFS 3.63 and CR 5.5

Managers, staff and childminders have a personal responsibility to manage safety every day. The EYFS outlines all providers, including childminders, who must assess:

- your premises and equipment – are they safe and suitable?
- your security systems – are they effective?
- supervision – are children effectively supervised by staff at all times?

A risk assessment policy should clearly outline a genuine intention to comply with all aspects of legislation and guidance.

For example:

- How potential hazards and risks associated with outdoor and indoor spaces, furniture, equipment and toys are identified and minimised.
- How policies and procedures are implemented, evaluated and reviewed.
- Accountability, roles and responsibilities. Is there a named person for health and safety?
- Who is responsible for checking systems and escalating concerns?

Policies and procedures are the starting point for managing health and safety including risk assessment in early years settings. However, written statements alone do not fulfil your health and safety obligations.

Common errors with risk assessment policies and practice in early years settings are:

- confusion; staff/individuals perceive daily check sheets as a risk assessment
- lack of clarity; staff/individuals are not aware of the policy detail or their roles/responsibilities
- ineffectiveness; written procedures adopted from elsewhere in order to comply with legal requirements but practice does not reflect written procedures.

Law

Refer to the definition of a 'competent person' in Chapter 3 when judging your staff and assigning roles regarding health and safety.

Remember

Ensure your documentation is personal to your setting, understood by all staff and reviewed regularly. Inspectors may sample your risk assessment policies and procedures and will expect all staff and individuals to be familiar with them.

Review process

 EYFS 3.63 and CR 5.5

The EYFS and Childcare Register requirements state that risk assessments must be reviewed regularly – at least once a year or more frequently as the need arises. It is crucial to investigate and analyse all accidents and incidents in order to be proactive in accident prevention.

By identifying the root cause of accidents, it is possible to put control measures in place to prevent reoccurrences. When examining the root cause of accidents think about:

- immediate cause
- contributing factors
- system failure.

Review and assess all accidents, by looking at time, location, age of child, equipment, documents and staff on duty. Look for patterns (hotspots and blind spots) to help eliminate future risks.

Hotspots could be accidents happening at:

- the same time of day
- to the same children
- when certain staff are on duty
- in the same area of a room or outdoors.

What about blind spots in your setting or childminding environment? Think about human factors again – people can become complacent in the same environment every day. Rotate people so they can check each other's rooms and areas of responsibility.

 Remember

By implementing changes immediately, you are demonstrating that you recognise potential hazards and risks, and plan accordingly. You must also communicate changes to your team. Everyone needs to be aware and then everyone can be accountable.

Written risk assessments

 EYFS 3.63 and CR 5.5

You need to identify, check and record all risks in relation to two specific aspects:

- your premises, both indoors and outdoors, including all furniture, equipment and toys
- all outings (this is covered in a separate chapter).

A risk assessment needs to:

- be valid
- be reviewed
- involve everyone
- comply with legislation
- be a starting point.

Paperwork only forms part of the risk assessment process. Daily safety check sheets are a control measure and can be used as a tool to help to identify hazards. However, it is not sufficient to just 'tick a box'. For example, recording doors and gates are locked and secure only reflects a moment in time as people sometimes forget to lock gates and children will try and open doors. Check all areas used by children, including the toilets and outdoors every day. This is especially important if you are using shared premises as new hazards can appear overnight, such as litter and broken washbasins.

 Remember

Your risk assessment needs to be a working document, everyone needs to know where it is and feel able to add to it. Are you confident that new staff, students, apprentices, childminding assistants and volunteers understand this process? An inspector may ask them. For more information, see Ofsted factsheet: 'Requirements for risk assessment' (ref 120334; Nov 2012) http://www.ofsted.gov.uk/ resources/factsheet-childcare-requirements-for-risk-assessments.

Specialist activities or events

 EYFS 3.63

The EYFS does not prescribe how to risk assess, just to ensure that the process is suitable and sufficient. This gives individuals the freedom to plan and organise an innovative and varied range of activities that involve risk taking, which is beneficial to children. Staff can use common sense and personal judgement to demonstrate that activities are risk assessed and the benefits outweigh the dangers.

Do you have any pets or visits from an animal specialist that may pose a hazard to children? Think about hazards posed by specific activities, such as woodworking or visiting farms. Then you need to evaluate the risks regarding likelihood and severity. Then balance these with the learning potential for children.

HSE have produced a useful information sheet 'Preventing or controlling ill health from animal contact at visitor attractions': http://www.hse.gov.uk/pubns/ais23.pdf.

Supervision and vigilance in practice

 EYFS 3.19, CR 5.1–CR 5.4

Supervision is not about preventing children from exploring and trying out new challenges. It is about staff being flexible, proportionate and proactive in keeping children safe from harm.

Review the environment and each room. Think about hazards, location of equipment, emergency exits etc. Be particularly alert if you share a building, has anything been moved or changed since children last used the area?

Staff learn with experience which children need extra support, particularly babies and toddlers who have an inner drive to explore, coupled with a limited sense of danger. Ensure there is sufficient, experienced, qualified staff on duty to adequately supervise all children.

Consider your staff's intentions, perceptions and distractions. Is their behaviour safe or unsafe?

Inspectors will assess a setting's attitude to promoting safe play including planning and observation that reflects children's individual achievements and targets. Safety equipment, such as stair gates, are not a substitute for staff vigilance and supervision.

Does everyone know who is inside, outside, who has just arrived or gone home? Think about staffing ratios, conducting regular head counts on children and how you record their attendance. For example, in a day care setting, if 12 children go outside to play, 12 children need to come back inside. Be alert to children who arrive late or go home early and make sure your attendance records reflect these changes.

Remember

Inspectors may count children during the inspection and then check attendance registers to ensure documents accurately represent the number of children on site. This gives an insight into how prepared you are if there was an emergency, such as a fire drill. Therefore, ensure your supervision procedures are robust and your audit systems are effective.

Minimising hazards and risks

 EYFS 3.19 and CR 5.5

Effective security systems are imperative in order to monitor access to your setting and prevent children from leaving the building. Remind adults to close doors behind them and monitor security throughout the day. Have you considered children's individual needs including age, maturity and behaviour when assessing risks?

Remember

Children are individual, unique and unpredictable! Inclusion needs to underpin all aspects of your practice. Inspectors will observe children's behaviour carefully, how everyone deals with situations and how safety is considered and relevant to each room, group of children and for childminders within the home environment.

In order to achieve ongoing, effective safety systems and facilitate children's sense of adventure, a professional, integrated approach to risk assessment is required. Hazard alerts can help you get a full picture of your setting's safety. Use a hazard alert system so anyone, such as parents, volunteers, visitors can notify a risk or hazard they may have noticed.

Remember

A 'fresh pair of eyes' can see things you do not. An inspector will be looking at childcare practice throughout, checking your safety systems and cross-referencing practice against policies and procedures to ensure children can play safely and access challenging activities. Do not rely on the inspector to be your hazard alert system as this will be reflected in your inspection grading.

Childminders

The above guidance applies to childminders who also need to consider:

 CR 5.5

Childminders must undertake an annual risk assessment of all premises and equipment. This must be updated to reflect any significant changes. Therefore, childminders must ensure any identified hazards and risks are controlled or removed including all hazards and risks within their home, garden and associated with daily activities.

For childminders, working in their own home means they are aware of potential hazards and dangers. However, complacency and the actions of other household members can compromise safety systems as the work space becomes a family home again once children have left. For example, household hazards, such as stair gates being moved or dangerous items, such as razors being left in bathrooms.

 CR 5.1

A daily check of your home prior to children arriving ensures hazards are spotted and safety systems reinstated, such as computer flexes made safe and stair gates reinstalled.

Ensure your risk assessment reflects any significant changes in the home environment. You are required to notify Ofsted of significant changes.

Examples include:

- any building or decorating work that impacts on children's well-being
- adults and anyone over 16 years old moving into the home
- additional features to the property, such as the installation of a garden pond.

Your own assessment

➡ The Management of Health and Safety at Work Regulations 1999 Regulation 3(1)(a)

An employer is required to carry out a suitable and sufficient assessment of risks to the health and safety of his employees while they are at work. This means looking at the workplace, equipment used and the activities that take place there and assessing how your staff might be harmed or hurt.

➡ The Management of Health and Safety at Work Regulations 1999 Regulation 3(1)(b)

The employer must consider the risks to which persons not in their employment, but who are affected by risks on the premises and within the business activities. This means:

- staff
- children
- visitors
- contractors.

Childminders

→ The Management of Health and Safety at Work Regulations 1999 Regulations 3(2)(a) and 3(2)(b)

Self-employed people also need to carry out a suitable and sufficient risk assessment of risks to their own health and safety while at work and risks to other people affected by their work.

Once risks have been identified, they must be controlled. This is your risk assessment. It is a tool to enable you to plan for and to manage health and safety.

 Remember

Think about real risks. In the banning of playing conkers in a school example, HSE advised that the health and safety risk to children playing with the conkers was insignificant/trivial and that any children deliberately hitting each other over the head with conkers was a discipline issue and not a health and safety issue.

There is guidance available at http://www.hse.gov.uk/risk/index.htm. This includes example risk assessments and frequently asked questions.

Definitions to help understand risk assessment

Consider some definitions that will help in this process. You need to think about your business and identify hazards.

A hazard is something that can cause harm, for example, hot water, cleaning chemicals and sharp surfaces.

Some examples of hazards in premises are:

- security of site
- hot surfaces/hot water, for example burns and scalds
- finger traps on doors, for example entrapment
- uneven surfaces, for example slips trips and falls
- glazing, for example, falls from height or cutting hazard
- blind cords, for example entanglement.

Some examples of hazards associated with equipment are:

- play equipment, for example, falls from a height
- toys, for example choking
- craft materials, for example choking
- cleaning equipment and chemicals, for example ingestion and contact
- catering equipment, for example burns and scalds.

Some hazards may be less obvious but are still important to consider in your risk assessments. These hazards can be associated with conditions, behaviour and both routine and non-routine activities.

Examples of hazards associated with human factors and activities are:

- administration of medicines, for example, unauthorised dose, use or overdose
- allergies, both general and food
- sick children or staff, for example infection
- outings and transporting children, for example loss of a child
- sleeping and naps, for example risk of cot death
- feeding children, for example choking.

Risk is the likelihood or chance of the harm occurring in your business operation. It considers:

- who may be harmed and how
- the consequences, severity or impact of the incident/accident.

A control measure is a safety precaution or procedure that if followed will reduce the likelihood of the incident or accident occurring. The law talks about preventative and protective measures.

A risk assessment is an evaluation of the hazards in your business:

- what could happen
- who might get hurt
- how severe the impact or consequences will be
- how likely it is that it will happen.

It considers your existing controls, measures or safety precautions in your business. It tells you if you are doing enough or what else you need to do.

A step by step approach to risk assessment

- Identify the **hazard**.
- Identify **who** may be harmed and **how**.
- Identify **what you are already doing** to control the risk, for example your safety precautions.
- Do you need to **take further action** or do anything else?
- Use an **action plan** to complete this work and sign it off.
- Remember to **review**.

Other health and safety laws require you to control risks, for example, the Manual Handling Operations Regulations 1992 (as amended). You need to consider and comply with these other health and safety requirements.

When undertaking risk assessments, it is important to talk to and involve staff. They are a vital source of information and can tell you what works well or not and what really happens in practice.

Also look at accident records including 'near misses'. These help you to identify hazards or problems in the workplace that you need to consider as part of your risk assessments.

HSE has devised a simple five step approach to risk assessment for small to medium size (SME) uncomplicated businesses. There is guidance and a template that can be used at http://www.hse.gov.uk/risk/index.htm.

Remember

The risk assessments need to apply to your premises and your work activity. They need to be relevant to your business operation. You can use HSE's example risk assessments as guidance but you should not copy them as your own, as you may overlook a significant risk in your business.

Risk assessment and 'competent persons'

 The Management of Health and Safety at Work Regulations 1999 Regulation 7(1)

You do not need a formal qualification to carry out a risk assessment but these regulations require that an employer appoint a competent person to assist in health and safety matters such as risk assessment. The 'competent person' is discussed in Chapter 3.

Consider whether you or someone inside your business has the skills to carry out the risk assessments. Information is available from a variety of sources, such as trade associations or HSE's website. If you do not think you have the skills then you may need to get help from a competent source outside of the business.

Even if you employ a consultant to help you no one knows your business as well as you and your staff do. So you and they need to be involved in this process. The most effective risk assessments are those where staff are actively involved in the process.

What is a suitable and sufficient risk assessment?

The law does not tell you what is suitable and sufficient, but guidance can be found at http://www.hse.gov.uk/risk/index.htm.

For an assessment to be suitable and sufficient you need to demonstrate that you have thought about the hazards and evaluated the risks in your business. Your risk assessment must show that you have thought about:

- the significant risks in your business
- all groups of people who may be harmed by these risks in your business, for example staff, children, visitors and contractors
- that you are taking reasonable precautions
- that the remaining level of risk when the safety precautions are followed is acceptable.

Remember

Significant risks are real risks. It is important not to get distracted by imaginary risks or by health and safety myths.

Evaluating risk

This is the part of risk assessment that seems to cause most worry and confusion. Some risks may be trivial and insignificant, in which case no further action will be required.

Other risks may be adequately controlled by your existing safety precautions and procedures and again you may not be required to take action at this point in time. If something changes at some point in the future you will need to review your assessment.

→ The Management of Health and Safety at Work Regulation 1999 Regulation 4

Where your risks are significant and you need to take action, the Management of Health and Safety at Work Regulations 1999 specify that where preventative and protective measures are implemented to control risk a principle known as the hierarchy of control should be applied.

You need to consider what do to:

- avoid the risk or if this is not practical or possible
- evaluate the risk through assessment and use preventative and protective measures to control and reduce the risk to the lowest level possible.

Some examples of preventative and protective measures are:

- working in a different way to eliminate or reduce risk
- physical measures such as guarding equipment
- health and safety precautions and procedures
- training staff
- use of personal protective equipment (PPE).

Remember

The greater the risk, the more robust your safety precautions need to be.

Recording significant findings of a risk assessment

→ The Management of Health and Safety at Work Regulations 1999 Regulations 3(6)(a) and 3(6)(b)

The regulations state that if you employ five or more employees then you record the significant findings of your risk assessment. You also need to record any group of employees who are especially at risk. You can record this in writing or electronically on a computer, as long as the information is accessible.

Your significant findings should include:

- a description of what you are assessing
- what the hazards are
- who can be hurt and how
- what safety procedures are already in place
- what else you need to do.

Implementing the findings of a risk assessment

Implement the findings of your risk assessments to control health and safety in your business by:

- prioritising what you need to do first
- devising an action plan to organise and to monitor completion of the work required.

Where the risk is high, you will need to deal with this first. High risk is where there is a high probability or probability that the incident or accident will occur and the consequences, severity or impact are extremely harmful or harmful, for example it may result in a reportable accident to staff or children.

Inform staff about your significant findings

➡ The Management of Health and Safety at Work Regulations 1999 Regulation 10(1)

You must inform staff about the findings including the safety precautions you are taking. This is regardless of whether the findings need to be recorded or not. This is an important part of the implementation and it is a legal requirement.

Check that staff understand and are following your safety procedures and precautions.

Monitor and review

Monitoring the effectiveness of your safety precautions and procedures is an important starting point to risk assessment and ongoing management control.

Risk assessments should not be desktop exercises – you need to assess what is actually happening in practice in the workplace, your working activities and procedures.

A useful way to continue to monitor that precautions and procedures are understood and followed is by conducting health and safety audits, recording and sharing the findings with staff and taking any necessary corrective action.

➡ The Management of Health and Safety at Work Regulations 1999 Regulations 3(3)(a) and 3(3)(b)

The law says that you should review your risk assessment if you think it is no longer valid. Or where there have been changes in the business activity or area to which the risk assessment relates. In this case you need to review your risk assessment to see if it is affected by changes and to see if your safety precautions are still adequate or whether you need to do more.

You need to review the risk assessments when things in the business change, for example, you bring in new equipment, or use another area of the premises.

Always review your risk assessment in the event of an accident or incident to see what action you could take to prevent this from happening again. If you did not have a risk assessment for the event or activity relating to the accident, use one to help you to investigate and to identify what precautions you need to put in place.

It is good practice to set a review date for the risk assessment on completion.

Groups of workers requiring further consideration

The Regulations consider specific groups of workers who require further consideration, including temporary workers, new or expectant mothers and young persons.

Guidance on the requirements for temporary workers and new or expectant mothers and young people can be found at http://www.hse.gov.uk/toolbox/workers/index.htm.

Young people

A young person is defined as someone who has not reached the age of 18. Before you employ a young person you must consider a number of factors in your risk assessment:

➡️ The Management of Health and Safety at Work Regulations 1999 Regulations 3(4) and 3(5)

- the inexperience, lack of awareness of risks and immaturity of the young person
- the layout of the workplace and the area where the young person will work
- the nature, degree and duration of exposure to physical, biological and chemical agents
- the form, range, and use of work equipment and the way in which it is handled
- organisation of processes and activities in the business
- the extent of the health and safety training provided or to be provided to young people.

Consider:

- what they will be doing
- where they will be working
- whether they will be using or working near equipment.

The Management of Health and Safety at Work Regulations 1999 Regulation 19(1)

An employer must ensure that young people at work are protected from risks to their health and safety arising from their lack of experience or a lack of awareness of existing hazards or potential hazards due to a lack of maturity.

Additionally consider:

- what training and supervision you need to give to the young person
- their awareness of your emergency procedures and their ability to respond in an emergency situation, for example, fire evacuation.

> **!** **Remember**
>
> A young person may need more training and supervision particularly when they first start working with you.

 The Management of Health and Safety at Work Regulations 1999 Regulation 19(2)

An employer must not employ a young person to do work if that work:

- is beyond their physical capability
- exposes them to harmful substances that have long-term effects on their health, for example toxic or cancer causing substances
- exposes them to radiation
- could result in a risk of accidents that they are unlikely to recognise because of immaturity, a lack of training or attention to safety
- involves a risk to safety due to extreme heat, cold, noise and vibration.

There are exceptions to this in certain circumstances provided the young person is over minimum school leaving age.

 The Management of Health and Safety at Work Regulations 1999 Regulation 19(3)

If the young person is over minimum school leaving age they may undertake elements of the restricted work for training purposes provided:

- the risk is reduced to the lowest level practicable
- a competent person supervises the young person.

 Law

Children under minimum school leaving age cannot be exposed to these restricted works whether they are employed or on work experience.

> **!** **Remember**
>
> You do not have to do a separate risk assessment for every young person that you employ but you should review the assessment if the work changes.

Children

A child is defined as a person of compulsory school age.

➜ The Management of Health and Safety at Work Regulations 1999 Regulations 10(2) and 10(3)

Before you employ a child, or allow that child to undertake work experience in your business you must advise their parents or legal guardian of the findings of your risk assessment and the safety precautions that are in place.

Work experience students will be classed as 'employees' under health and safety law.

You should also check with your local council as there may be other restrictions imposed under child welfare laws including what children can do, how long they can work and the need to get written permission from the parent or legal guardian.

There is more information about the employment of young people on HSE's website at http://www.hse.gov.uk/youngpeople/risks/.

Shared workplaces

➜ The Management of Health and Safety at Work Regulations 1999 Regulation 11

Where workplaces are used by more than one employer or are shared by an employer and a self-employed person, there must be arrangements in place for the cooperation and coordination of health and safety matters.

This is to ensure that:

- shared risks are dealt with
- each party is aware of risks involved in the other business that may affect them and their employees
- emergency procedures, such as fire evacuation are put in place.

Working in a host workplace

➜ The Management of Health and Safety at Work Regulations 1999 Regulation 12

The host employer or host self-employed person must ensure that people not in their employment receive information about the risks to their health and safety and the preventative and protective measures in place while they are at work in the host premises. This may be done by giving information directly to the person or to their employer.

If the information is given to the employer, then checks must be made to ensure that this has been passed to the visiting worker and that they understand the information.

Both requirements in Regulations 11 and 12 aim to ensure that all parties meet their duties under health and safety law.

 Remember

Following a consultation HSE's publication 'Management of Health and Safety at Work Regulations 1999. Approved Code of Practice & guidance,' series Code L21 has been withdrawn. Guidance is now provided on HSE's website by following the links given.

8 Accidents

An accident is a sequence of unplanned events that may or may not result in injury or loss. In this definition it is important to consider 'near misses', where something happened but no one was injured or no damage was done, as an accident. Most accidents are preventable with the application of practical risk management techniques. The key to accident prevention is risk assessment and this is why risk assessment is such a central theme of health and safety law. When a serious accident occurs, it can have life-changing and catastrophic consequences for the accident victim, their family, the employer, staff and local community. This can include subsequent enforcement action by both the enforcing authority and Ofsted.

The EYFS requirements for this section must be read in conjunction with the health and safety requirements to ensure all obligations are fulfilled. The EYFS encourages children to take responsibility for their personal safety and to learn about and to take controlled risks. Unfortunately, where tragedies have occurred, serious care reviews often highlight major shortfalls in professionalism, duty of care and non-compliance with legislation. Providers must adhere to the guidance on notifications to ensure they have fulfilled their legal duties.

Accident recording and investigation are important risk management tools that should be used to learn from these events by identifying what went wrong and why. This enables review and improvements to be made. There are also legal duties to notify certain types of accidents/incidents under the EYFS and under health and safety law. The Reporting of Injuries, Diseases and Dangerous Occurrences Regulations 2013 (RIDDOR) came into force on 1 October 2013 and replaced the old regulations (RIDDOR 1995 (as amended). They specify what types of accident/incidents require reporting and the time frames in which the report needs to be made. The duty to notify, what to notify and the timescales for notification differ between EYFS and RIDDOR and both notifications need to be made. This chapter summarises the requirements of both the EYFS and health and safety law, providing clear and concise advice on how to notify to meet both sets of requirements.

Notification of accidents

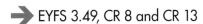 EYFS 3.49, CR 8 and CR 13

The EYFS outlines that all serious accidents, illnesses, injuries or death of children while in the care of a setting must be notified to Ofsted and local child protection agencies. Notifications need to be as soon as is reasonably practicable, but within 14 days of any situation arising. Failure to comply with this requirement is an offence.

➡ EYFS 3.48 and CR 8

Ensure accident recording is detailed, legible and well written. Spelling errors and poor grammar can detract from the main issues and remember your records may be called upon as evidence if a case goes to court. It is good practice to examine the circumstances surrounding an accident in order to prevent reoccurrence. For example, your conclusion may be that staff need to be deployed differently or require more training. You may decide to remove or relocate specific equipment. Whatever the circumstances, you need to be able to demonstrate that all accidents are reviewed as part of your preventative measures.

Children's behaviour

 EYFS 3.2, EYFS 3.50–EYFS 3.52, CR 6.2 and CR 6.3

All children are individual, unique and unpredictable. Staff need to consider children's ages, behaviour and inclusion in all aspects of health and safety. For example, new children coming into a setting, children with behaviour or other special needs may need additional supervision when using tools, equipment and on outings.

Behaviour and stages of development

EYFS 3.2 and EYFS 3.50–EYFS 3.52, CR 6.2 and CR 6.3

Babies and young children have an inbuilt desire to explore their surroundings and initially have little sense of danger. As children develop, they learn and adopt a sense of self-protection, providing they have opportunities to make safe choices and try new challenges. Children need to be engaged, motivated and encouraged to think in order to support learning across all areas, including risk taking.

Behaviour and suitability of premises and equipment

CR 5.1 and CR 6.3

Your setting needs to be a safe environment for children to thrive. Organisation is key, for example, how you deploy staff, equipment and resources. Give children a sense of ownership – providing a clipboard, safety hats and a pen, helps to make health and safety fun and can be revealing in what children identify as potential hazards. These observations are good evidence to include in children's development charts.

Children's behaviour and development play a crucial part in accident prevention. The characteristics of effective learning in the EYFS are highlighted below:

- playing and exploring – engagement
- active learning – motivation
- creating and thinking critically – thinking.

'Unique child' outlines the importance of children learning by trial and error. Staff can support children through detailed planning, organisation and clear intervention boundaries. Staff should embrace spontaneous learning opportunities, such as a fresh snowfall. Help children take responsibility for their own safety. For example, reminding them to dress appropriately for weather, hats and gloves etc.

Encourage children to try new activities and judge risks for themselves. Staff need to be positive both in feedback to children and in body language. It can be difficult to stay calm and encouraging when watching a child on a climbing frame, but children need to challenge their own limits in order to develop a sense of danger and also achievement. Talk through children's ideas and ambitions with them, as your support and encouragement will enable them to be creative and take a risk.

> **Childminders**
>
> The above guidance applies to childminders who also need to consider:
>
> EYFS 3.3
>
> You will need to assess your home environment daily to ensure children can play safely.

Accidents

Accidents are unplanned events that arise from one or more of a number of conditions. These can be human factors, such as tiredness, boredom, and lack of awareness, inexperience and behaviour. The conditions in the work environment such as uneven floor surfaces, steps, lack of lighting, defective toys, equipment and conditions to do with the job, such as repetitive tasks, requirement for regular manual handling of objects, people and children.

Risk assessment and providing your employees with information, instruction, training and supervision are important elements in accident prevention.

Accident investigation

Another tool that is often overlooked in accident prevention is accident investigation. When an accident occurs in your setting it is important to investigate what happened and to try to prevent the same thing from happening again. This is why it is important to have a system in place to report and record any accidents.

When reporting and recording accidents you need to consider and record 'near misses'. Those occurrences where something happened but no injury or damage resulted. This type of incident should be treated in the same way as an accident. By reporting, recording and investigating near misses you can take action to prevent a more serious accident resulting in injury or damage occurring.

- Report accidents or 'near misses'.
- Record the details of what happened.
- Gather the facts about what happened.
- Analyse the information to identify the cause(s).

- Review the information and consider how you can prevent a further occurrence.
- Implement corrective action.
- Involve your staff in this process and keep them advised.

Staff should know what to do when an accident occurs, the accident reporting system and how to use it to report and record accidents. This information needs to be reviewed so an accident investigation can take place. Any risk assessment that relates to what happened should be reviewed as part of this investigation process.

Recording accidents

➜ The Social Security (Claims and Payments) Regulations 1979

If you are an employer and you employ more than 10 people you are required to keep an accident book.

An accident book is used for recording accidents, injuries and incidents. This law has been amended to allow you to keep the accident record electronically as long as you can retrieve this information.

➜ The Reporting of Injuries, Diseases and Dangerous Occurrences Regulations 2013 (RIDDOR) Regulation 12

There are other laws relating to accident reporting that also require you as the 'responsible person', to keep records of certain types of accidents, incidents and work-related diseases. These regulations are known as the Reporting of Injuries, Diseases and Dangerous Occurrences Regulations 2013 also known as RIDDOR.

RIDDOR details the types of injuries, incidents and occupational illnesses that you have to notify to your enforcing authority regardless of the size of your business.

Your enforcing authority is the body that would inspect your business to see that it meets health and safety requirements. This will be either your local Environmental Health Department or HSE.

Childminders

RIDDOR applies to self-employed people at work.

Given the requirements of the various regulations it is recommended that no matter how large or small your business, you have a system in place for recording accidents, 'near misses', incidents and cases of occupational illnesses.

This includes a system to record all of the above whether they involve your staff, your children, visitors or contractors who have an accident or are involved in an incident within your business.

What to record in an accident book/ accident form

 RIDDOR 2013 Regulation 12 and Schedule 1 Parts 1 and 2

The law requires you to keep records of work-related deaths, reportable injuries, over three day injuries, dangerous occurrences and reportable occupational illnesses for three years from the date when the record was made.

In general, the following details need to be recorded in relation to any accident or incident.

- Date and time of the accident or incident.
- Details about the injured employee:
    - full name
    - occupation
    - nature of injury.
- Details of the injured person (if accident involves a person not at work):
    - full name
    - status (for example, 'customer', 'visitor' or 'children')
    - nature of injury.
- Place where the accident or incident happened.
- A brief description of the circumstances in which the accident or incident happened.
- Date when the accident or incident was notified to the enforcing authority.
- How the notification was made to the enforcing authority.

Many accident books or forms also provide space to give detail of the type of first aid administered and details of the first aider. It is also a good idea to make a note of the details of any witnesses to the accident.

 Remember

You must keep all personal information safe.

Reportable accidents

 RIDDOR 2013

Under these Regulations the 'responsible person' has a duty to notify certain types of accident, incident or occupational illness that occur at work, to the enforcing authority.

The definition of the responsible person can change depending on circumstances. In most cases and certainly when notifying accident to an employee, the responsible person is the employer.

Certain accidents and injuries that can involve 'persons not at work' are also reportable. In your business such people would be the children in your care and any visitors who are at your business in connection with it. In this case, the person in control of the premises and the business activity taking place there at the time of the accident, is the responsible person.

If the injured person is a self-employed worker then the responsible person can change depending where the accident took place.

If the accident takes places involving a self-employed person at work in premises where the self-employed person is not on their own business premises, then the accident needs to be notified by the person in control of the premises and the work activity taking place.

If the self-employed person is working in premises, that are under their own control, then they are the responsible person to make the notification. The notification can also be made by someone on their behalf.

Reportable accidents to 'persons at work'

The responsible person must notify the following types of injury to their employees that arise from an accident at work.

 RIDDOR 2013 Regulation 6

Work-related fatalities

All deaths arising out of, or in connection with, work whether or not that person died at the workplace.

There is also a requirement in the case of an employee to notify any death that occurs as a result of an injury, even if the death occurs up to a year after the accident has taken place. This is in addition to any previous notification made at the time that the accident took place.

 RIDDOR 2013 Regulation 4(1)

Non-fatal injuries to workers.

These are also called 'specified injuries' in the guide to the new regulations:

- any bone fracture diagnosed by a registered medical practitioner, other than to a finger, thumb or toe
- amputation of an arm, hand, finger, thumb, leg, foot or toe
- any injury diagnosed by a registered medical practitioner as being likely to cause permanent blinding or reduction in sight in one or both eyes
- any crush injury to the head or torso causing damage to the brain or internal organs in the chest or abdomen
- any burn injury (including scalding) that covers more than 10 per cent of the whole body's total surface area; or causes significant damage to the eyes, respiratory system or other vital organs
- any degree of scalping requiring hospital treatment
- loss of consciousness caused by head injury or asphyxia
- any other injury arising from working in an enclosed space that leads to hypothermia or heat-induced illness; or requires resuscitation or admittance to hospital for more than 24 hours.

Remember

These types of injuries relate to people at work. This will mainly be your employees. However if a self-employed contractor has an accident while working at your premises, you need to make the notification as you are in control of the premises and the work activity.

Notifying a death or a non-fatal injury to workers

In the case of a death or one of the specified injuries the responsible person needs to make the notification to the enforcing authority by the 'quickest practicable means'.

This means a telephone call to the Incident Contact Centre on 0845 300 9923 (opening hours Monday to Friday 8.30 am to 5 pm).

The telephone notification must be followed up by the completion and submission of an online notification form, which must be received within 10 days of the accident occurring. This form is called 'Report of an Injury'.

You will receive a copy of this form once you have submitted it online. Keep this for your records. It is your record of the reportable accident and notification. You can find advice at http://www.hse.gov.uk/riddor/report.htm.

Details for notifications out of hours are also given on this website.

Changes to the law on reportable injuries

Since 6 April 2012, there has been a change to what are known as 'over three days injuries' to persons at work where they are incapacitated for over three consecutive days as a result of an accident at work. Prior to this date these injuries were reportable and required the completion and submission of a written notification to the enforcing authority within 10 days of the accident date.

Since the change you are still required to keep a record of this type of accident but you are not required to notify it. You need to record in your accident book and ensure you have the following details:

- date and time of the accident
- particulars of the injured person – full name, occupation and nature of injury
- place where the accident happened
- a brief description of the circumstances in which the accident happened.

Reportable 'over seven day' injuries

 RIDDOR 2013 Regulation 4(2)

The requirement to report the 'over three day injury' to the enforcing authority has been replaced by the requirement to notify an injury that results in the incapacity of a person at work for more than seven consecutive days.

When calculating the consecutive incapacity days you need to consider non-work days, such as days off shift, weekends, holidays or when the injured person was not due to work anyway. Ask the injured person to confirm whether if they had to work, they would have been able to do so. If they were not capable of working or carrying out their normal duties on these non-work days, you need to include these days when calculating the 'over seven day period' and the over 'three day period'. You do not include the day of the accident when calculating the consecutive days.

You also need to consider 'light duties'. If an employee is unable to carry out their full range of duties for more than seven consecutive days as a result of an accident at work, then it is a reportable injury. While the report needs to be made within 15 days of the accident, you also need to consider instances where the injured person does not become incapacitated straight after the accident.

If the incapacity develops later and results in a more than seven consecutive days absence from work, then the report must be made within 15 days of that absence.

How to make a notification of an 'over seven day injury'

The telephone notification is not required. The responsible person must complete and submit the online notification form that must be received within 15 days of the accident occurring. This form is called Report of an Injury.

You will receive a copy of this form once you have submitted it online. Keep this for your records. It is your record of the reportable accident and notification.

You can find advice at http://www.hse.gov.uk/riddor/report.htm.

Incidents of non-consensual violence to employees

 RIDDOR 2013 Regulation 2(1)

Incidents of non-consensual violence to people at work fall under the definition of an accident. Therefore, if your employee is subjected to a violent incident at work where physical injury results, the accident may be reportable if:

- the injury is a specified injury or death
- the member of staff is incapacitated for more than seven consecutive days as a result of the injury.

Reportable accidents to 'persons not at work'

→ RIDDOR 2013 Regulations 5, 6 and Schedule 1 Parts 1 and 2

This type of accident affects your children and visitors to your premises. These people although not at work are affected by your business activity.

- Work-related fatalities to non-workers

All deaths arising out, of or in connection with, work whether or not that person died at the workplace.

- Other types of reportable injury to 'persons not at work'

Under the new regulations, this type of injury is called a 'non-fatal injuries to non-workers'. If such a person has an accident while on your premises, and is taken from the site where the accident happened to hospital for treatment for an injury, then this is a reportable accident and the responsible person must notify it to the enforcing authority.

This is regardless of how the injured person is taken to hospital whether by car, taxi, ambulance and so on. The accident is still reportable whether treatment at hospital is given or not. There is no requirement to confirm what treatment has been given.

However, if no injury is apparent and the accident victim is taken to hospital as a precaution only, then current guidance states that there is no requirement to notify.

The notification process for this type of accident is the same as for a death or a specified injury to a person at work.

Dangerous occurrences

→ RIDDOR 2013 Regulation 7, Schedules 1 and 2

There are certain types of incidents that occur that also require notification under RIDDOR. These may seem unlikely to occur in your business but you need to be aware of them.

Dangerous occurrences are listed in the regulations and an example is:

- the collapse of, the overturning of, or the failure of any load-bearing part of any lift or hoist.

Occupational diseases

→ RIDDOR 2013 Regulation 8 Schedule 1 Part 1

RIDDOR also details certain types of illnesses that can develop through exposure to occupational hazards in the workplace. These are known as occupational diseases.

Law

The new regulations aim to simplify the requirements placed on businesses. There have been changes to the list of specified injuries, incidents and diseases that you are required to notify. Previous guidance on RIDDOR 1995 (as amended) has been replaced to reflect these changes.

HSE has also produced a simple guide called 'Reporting accidents and incidents at work. A brief guide to the Reporting of Injuries, Diseases and Dangerous Occurrences Regulations 2013 (RIDDOR).'

You can obtain this and other up-to-date information on RIDDOR by visiting HSE's website at http://www.hse.gov. uk/riddor.

An example of an occupational disease listed in the regulations is 'occupational dermatitis, where the person's work involves significant or regular exposure to a known skin sensitizer or irritant', RIDDOR 2013 Regulation 8(c).

Where a written diagnosis by a medical practitioner is received in relation to a worker, then a notification must be made to the enforcing authority.

There is guidance about dangerous occurrences and occupational diseases and how to notify them on HSE's website at http://www.hse. gov.uk/riddor/report.htm. The site also contains the forms on which a dangerous occurrence and occupational diseases can be notified.

Remember

It is an offence under the Health and Safety at Work Etc. Act 1974 to fail to comply with health and safety regulations. Therefore if you fail to notify a reportable accident, incident or occupational disease as required under RIDDOR you are committing an offence. Late reporting is also an offence and you may be prosecuted in both circumstances.

This is regardless of whether you have notified Ofsted and met your separate EYFS requirements.

9 First aid

First aid is the assistance given to a casualty by a trained first aider to preserve life and/or to prevent a condition, injury or illness from becoming worse while awaiting medical attention from a medical professional. It is also the treatment of minor injuries, for example cuts, that do not require medical attention. It is an essential requirement to the operation of a safe business, regardless of the size of the setting.

Children thrive in environments where they are healthy, happy and their individual needs are met. Promoting children's good health is a fine balance between professionalism, partnership working and prompt intervention. The EYFS outlines the minimum requirements to ensure children receive prompt, appropriate attention in the event of an accident or emergency. All settings must ensure an appointed, qualified first aider who holds a valid certificate is on-site at all times. The requirements are very specific and complement the risk-based health and safety regulations relating to first aid. These requirements must be met in conjunction with the Health and Safety (First Aid) Regulations 1981 (as amended). The main focus of the childcare sector is that children and the first aid requirements for adults and children differ significantly. This is why the EYFS stipulates that 'first aid training must be local authority approved and relevant for workers caring for young children'. This is interpreted as paediatric first aid training.

The Health and Safety (First Aid) Regulations 1981, were subject to certain change that came into effect on 1 October 2013. From this date first aid training providers and first aid qualifications no longer require approval from HSE. Guidance has been reissued to reflect these changes. The regulations are still known as The Health and Safety (First Aid) Regulations 1981. The changes aim to simplify matters for business and to increase the range of first aid training provision available to businesses.

The regulations still require that first aid provision be based on an assessment of the needs of the business. This chapter will guide you through the requirements of the EYFS and give a broad outline of the health and safety requirements specified in law.

Training

 EYFS 3.24 and CR 1.3

Deployment of staff and validity of certificates are two areas that often compromise inspection outcomes for providers. There must be at least one person who is a qualified first aider on site at all times, whenever children are present. Any outings children participate in must be organised to ensure children can be treated in the event of an accident of emergency by qualified first aiders. All first aid training must be local authority approved and is usually a minimum of 12 hours' tuition.

Sickness procedures

➔ EYFS 3.42, EYFS 3.43, EYFS 3.44 and CR 8

Staff must be aware of how to respond to children who arrive or become ill/infectious while at a setting. Up-to-date contact details for parents and carers must be kept on file. Sickness procedures including exclusion periods must be discussed and made clear to parents and carers as they will need to make alternative childcare arrangements when their children are ill.

Medication policy

➔ EYFS 3.43 and CR 8

Documentation relating to administration of medication must reflect required dosage and why a child requires medication. For more advice, see Ofsted factsheet: 'Giving medication to children in registered childcare' (Ref 080290; January 2013). If the administration requires technical knowledge, such as an Epipen, please refer to the health and safety section of this book for further guidance.

Permissions and recording

➔ EYFS 3.44 and CR 8

Written permission from the child's parents and carer must be obtained before administering any medicine (prescription or non-prescription) to a child. Medication records must be completed every time medication is administered. Documentation must outline that parents and carers are informed on a daily basis or as soon as is reasonably practicable. Informing parents and carers promptly about administered medication is crucial in order to avoid an inadvertent overdose, which could be fatal for a child.

Treatment and procedures

➔ EYFS 3.48 and CR 8

There must be an accessible first aid box available at all times that can be used with children. 'Accessible' is the key word here. It is usual to have a box for each base room in a larger setting and/or a main first aid box located in the office. Boxes need to be instantly recognisable; the international standard is an equal white cross on a green background.

Remember

It is important to check the contents of all first aid boxes. This includes any first aid boxes kept in minibuses or cars. Childminders should also check the contents of first aid boxes in their homes, as other household members may remove items inadvertently.

Records to be kept

 EYFS 3.48 and CR 8

All injuries, accidents and first aid administered to children must be clearly recorded. Ensure all staff are aware of what information must be included on accident records, such as date, time, injury, location of accident and witnesses.

Remember

Accident records must be completed in pen not pencil. Include full names of children and staff as these are official records that may be called upon as evidence.

Parents and carers must be informed at the earliest opportunity of any accidents or injuries sustained by their children. This may be required immediately in the event of an emergency or when children are collected if the injury or treatment is minor.

Childminders

The above guidance applies to childminders who also need to consider the following:

 EYFS 3.24 and CR 1.2

Childminders must hold a current paediatric first aid certificate before they can start caring for children. Childminders must ensure that any appointed assistants, who have sole charge of children for short periods of time, hold a current paediatric first aid certificate.

Sole charge of children by assistants must be agreed with Ofsted and by prior arrangement with parents and carers. Short periods of time could be interpreted as covering for a school collection. For further information on assistants, see Ofsted factsheet: 'Childminders using assistants' (January 2012, No. 080289).

 CR 8

All accidents and any medicine administered to children must be clearly recorded.

Health and Safety (First Aid) Regulations 1981

→ Health and Safety (First Aid) Regulations 1981 Regulation 3(1)

The requirements for employers and self-employed persons to make suitable first aid provision for employees and themselves in the workplace are contained within these regulations.

First aid requirements for your workplace are dependent upon your assessment. You need to consider:

- hazards presented by your business that have been highlighted in your risk assessments
- number of people you employ
- location of your workplace in relation to accident and emergency units
- any lone or off-site working by employees
- whether members of the public have access to your workplace
- any employees or children who have any special needs
- what type of accidents have occurred in your workplace.

You do not need to record your first aid assessment in writing but it is good practice to do so.

Remember

Although the requirements of the law are for first aid provision for employees and self-employed people, you should also consider the needs of your children and the public when assessing what level of first aid provision is required.

There is guidance that accompanies the first aid regulations. This contains advice on how to comply with the law: 'First aid at work. The Health and Safety (First-Aid) Regulations 1981. Guidance on Regulation' series code L74 and is available for download or purchase at http://www.hse.gov.uk/pubns/books/l74.htm. This guidance incorporates the previous Approved Code of Practice (ACOP) and reflects the current changes made to the law.

HSE's website also contains a First Aid Assessment Tool that will take you through a number of questions to help you to assess what is required in your business. This can be accessed at http://www.hse.gov.uk/firstaid/index.htm.

Law

Although first aid law puts the emphasis on your assessment and judgement, the EYFS contains very specific requirements for first aid provision and training.

Childminders

→ Health and Safety (First Aid) Regulations 1981 Regulation 5

The requirement to provide first aid provision applies to all workplaces including the home. A self-employed person must provide first aid equipment for their own use at work. You must also consider the needs of the children in your care.

First aid requirements

 Health and Safety (First Aid) Regulations 1981 Regulations 3(1), 3(2), 3(3) and 3(4)

The type of first aid provision can and will vary according to your assessment and includes:

- equipment, for example first aid kit
- facilities, for example first aid room
- first aiders who have attended an approved training course and hold a valid certificate of competence in first aid at work (FAW). This includes emergency first aid and first aid treatment
- appointed 'persons'.

A first aider:

- has attended an approved training course in first aid at work
- holds a valid certificate of competence.

This enables them to administer certain types of first aid, as per their qualification.

First aid training courses are available covering emergency first aid at work (EFAW).

An appointed person is appointed by the employer to take charge in an emergency situation. They ensure that emergency assistance is summonsed by calling the emergency services. They will also look after first aid equipment and facilities, for example, making sure that the first aid containers are available and are kept topped up with the correct materials.

Appointed persons should not administer first aid unless they have been trained to do so.

> **!** **Remember**
>
> You may need to plan first aid cover for shift work patterns and holidays.

First aid training

As part of the changes to the regulations your first aid training provider no longer needs to be approved by HSE, but you do need to ensure that they are competent. HSE has provided guidance on how to select a training provider depending on your first aid needs assessment. This guide 'Selecting a first-aid training provider. 'A guide for employers' HSE information sheet' is available at http://www.hse.gov.uk/pubns/geis3.htm.

The content of first aid training courses is provided by HSE and is contained in the guidance on regulation.

A certificate of competence in first aid expires after three years. If renewed before the expiry date or 28 days after this date, then the first aider can attend a shorter first aid refresher course.

If the training is not completed within this period then guidance recommends that a full first aid course is be completed again to resume first aider status.

HSE recommends that first aiders attend an annual refresher course to provide an update, as information and first aid techniques can change.

First aid equipment

The law does not list what needs to be inside a first aid container. HSE has produced guidance that details the type of contents in a low risk workplace. This includes a list of contents inside the box, individually wrapped plasters and various types of dressings, safety pins and disposable gloves.

The leaflet 'First aid at work. Your questions answered' is available at http://www.hse.gov.uk/pubns/indg214.pdf.

Your specialised first aid training will outline recommended first aid kit contents for dealing with children.

Your first aid assessment will tell you what you need in your business; however, medicines, tablets and so on should not be kept in first aid containers.

Having assessed your first aid provision you need to make your employees aware of the first aid equipment, facilities and arrangements that you have in place. Provide information about the location of the first aid container and identifying who are the first aiders/appointed persons. Some workplaces use posters or information on a notice board to provide this information.

Sterile eye wash bottles and dressings have a shelf life or date when they should be used by or replaced. This is marked on the bottle or the outer wrapping of the dressing.

Checking the first aid container is a responsibility of the appointed person or the first aider.

First aid treatment

In childcare you may have to deal with children who have allergies. Allergic reactions, such as anaphylactic shock can be life threatening. A first aider who is trained to use an Epipen can administer it in an emergency, provided that it is prescribed to that casualty.

Remember

Ask all parents and carers about their child's allergies.

The first aid regulations do not require you to keep a record of first aid administered but it is good practice to do so. The requirements of the Early Years Foundations Stage do require records to be kept and for parents and carers to be informed.

If the first aid was administered because of an accident, then this should be recorded in the accident book. You can combine these records and use the accident book for both purposes, to record accidents, incidents and any details of any first aid given.

Law

You can keep up to date about the changes to first aid at work and other health and safety laws at http://www.hse.gov.uk/news/index.htm.

10 Outings

The EYFS encourages providers to include a varied learning experience for all children that includes the outdoors. Outings contribute significantly to children's development. They give children opportunities to be adventurous, enjoy fresh air and exercise, share new experiences with their peer group and develop a sense of personal safety. Adults have a duty to ensure all children's safety on outings in order for children to enjoy challenging and enriching experiences. Providers need to ensure children are kept safe on outings. In this chapter, the EYFS requirements for safe outings are explained. It outlines what needs to be in place for outings to take place. The legal duties of an employer and a self-employed person under health and safety law are considered in the context of the children's health and safety.

Many myths surround health and safety rules about outings, due to uncertainty and misunderstanding about what is required under the EYFS and health and safety law. Providers may be concerned about planning and undertaking outings with their children. HSE recognises these concerns, balanced with the benefit of outings and have provided guidance for schools and local authority run establishments where they enforce health and safety matters.

Children's safety on outings

 EYFS 3.64

It is crucial that you consider children's age and stage of development when planning outings. Most outings are regular, short trips within the local community to places such as the library, local shops, parks and places of worship. Therefore, once you have identified the hazards, you can judge if this assessment needs to be in writing.

Full day trips to places such as a zoo, farm, seaside or activity centre obviously pose a range of different hazards. It is important to visit places beforehand if possible and seek advice from establishments as to the suitability of their premises and location for the age range of children you are taking. Many establishments have risk assessments that can be obtained prior to visits. It is important to share all of this pre-visit planning with parents and carers so they are in possession of the full facts before signing consent forms.

 Remember

While the hazards may be the same for regular, familiar outings, taking a different age range of children, different staff or different weather conditions can pose different hazards.

What to bring? This can be dependent upon the age of the children and where you are visiting, but a usual list might be:

- emergency contact details
- children's specific information, date of birth, immunisations etc.
- mobile phone, charged and in working order
- money
- first aid kit
- medication for specific children such as inhalers and Epipen
- wipes/anti-bacterial gel
- drinks/snacks
- weather clothes: hats, gloves
- nappies
- spare pants, change of clothes.

Ratios

 EYFS 3.64

Minimum staffing requirements must be met at all times, including on outings. Most settings choose to exceed minimum requirements on outings by requesting assistance from parents and volunteers.

Remember

The person in charge is responsible for ensuring the suitability of all volunteers in your setting and must take overall responsibility for the organisation of trips and outings.

All children need to be supervised at all times and this can be more challenging when children are excited and wanting to explore new surroundings. Also, if babies and toddlers are taken on trips there needs to be sufficient staff on duty for pushing children in prams or pushchairs.

Written permission

 EYFS 3.64

Parents and carers must be fully informed about any situations where their children are taken off-site. Signed consents must be obtained for every child prior to any outings taking place. It is important to do this in order to ensure you have the correct contact details for children's parents and carers for the specific day and time of the outing, just in case of an emergency.

Assessing risks and hazards

 EYFS 3.64 and CR 5.5

Planning is the key to successful outings. Be prepared and anticipate potential difficulties you might encounter. This includes a risk assessment of the journey/proposed route. In making a judgement about what needs to be in writing it is worth considering how you will evidence that you have anticipated risks and how you have shared this information with parents and carers.

Remember

Have an explicit policy and procedure to be followed in the event of a child going missing and discuss strategies with staff prior to undertaking outings. See Chapter 5 for more information on missing children.

Potential hazards to consider:

- weather
- surfaces – wet, slippery, icy, cobbled/uneven paving
- traffic
- roadworks
- other pedestrians
- cyclists
- mobility scooters
- wasps and bees
- dogs
- plants
- nettles, berries and thorns.

Risks to consider:

- sunburn
- slips, trips, falls
- road accidents
- accidents/injuries caused by collisions
- abduction
- violence
- animal bites
- animal stings
- anaphylaxis
- plants: scratches, stings, poisoning.

Remember

Refer to the Ofsted factsheet; 'Requirements for risk assessment' (Ref. 120334; November 2012) which includes outings; http://www.ofsted.gov.uk/resources/factsheet-childcare-requirements-for-risk-assessments.

For more advice on poisonous plants see: RHS, Potentially harmful garden plants. http://www.rhs.org.uk/Gardening/Sustainable-gardening/.../c_and_e_harmf.

For more advice on sun safety see: http://www.sunsafenurseries.co.uk/.

Insurance

 EYFS 3.65

Ensure any drivers and vehicles are fully insured for transporting children on outings. Vehicles need to be in a roadworthy condition and conform to legislation regarding child seat and seat belts. Reputable coach companies can provide evidence of driver and vehicle suitability.

If you use your own minibus, ensure the driver has undergone a Disclosure and Barring Service (DBS) check and that you are satisfied they are suitable and experienced in driving minibuses.

Ensure your policies and procedures for drivers outline sanctions for:

- speeding
- drink driving
- drug driving
- not using seat belts
- using mobile phones while driving
- driving while fatigued.

 Remember

It is important to undertake a safety check of your vehicle, prior to making every journey. ROSPA have a useful checklist available on their website: http://www.rospa.com › Advice & Information › Minibus Safety.

Childminders

The above guidance applies to childminders who also need to consider the following.

Accident planning is important, especially when transporting children in your own car. It is useful to carry identification and information to alert the emergency services that the passengers in your car are childminded children and you will have different emergency contact information for every child.

General health and safety duty

 HSWA 1974 Section 3(1)

The health and safety law covering outings is the general duty placed on an employer under this Act. This places a duty on the employer to ensure that people who are not employed but are affected by the activities of business are protected, so far as is reasonably practicable from risks to their health and safety.

- 'Persons not in employment'.

Children, accompanying parents, guardians, carers and other volunteers who may help on trips will come under this category.

 HSWA 1974 Section 2(1)

An employer also has a responsibility to ensure so far as is reasonably practicable the health, safety and welfare of their employees at work.

Risk assessment

→ The Management of Health and Safety at Work Regulations 1999 Regulation 3(1)

There are also requirements under these regulations for an employer to make a suitable and sufficient assessment of the risks to health and safety of their employees at work and people not in their employment but affected by the work activity.

The same law applies to other employers, so where you are visiting an establishment as part of an outing, they are required to look after visitor safety and to undertake risk assessments.

The requirement to record the significant findings or conclusions of a risk assessment or to have a written health and safety policy applies to businesses where five or more people are employed. Not all businesses you deal with will be required to have written systems but they are required to undertake risk assessments and to have suitable precautions in place.

Risk assessment is discussed in Chapter 7.

> **!** **Remember**
>
> It is important to teach children about risk.

For simple outings, you can involve the children in the risk assessment process, for example:

- identifying the hazards to be aware of when crossing the road and the safety precautions to be taken
- teaching the importance of hand washing after petting animals.

Childminders

 HSWA 1974 Section 3(2)

→ The Management of Health and Safety at Work Regulations 1999 Regulation 3(2)

As self-employed people, although the sections of the law are different the responsibility is the same.

A self-employed person has a responsibility to look after their own health and safety while at work.

Law

More complex leisure activities are covered by a set of regulations known as the Adventure Activities Licensing Regulations 2004. They require certain providers of facilities for adventure activities to be licensed (paid provision of four defined adventure activities – trekking, water sports, caving and climbing – for young people less than 18 years old).

These regulations are not considered in the context of the childcare sector covered by this book. They have recently been the subject of a consultation, so may be subject to change in the future.

11 Food safety

The EYFS highlights physical development as a 'Prime Area of Learning'. This outlines the importance of children developing healthy lifestyles and enjoying a balanced, healthy diet. It is crucial that the EYFS section is read in conjunction with the food and safety law component, as both sets of requirements must be fulfilled.

Food safety legislation requires that food premises are registered and meet certain basic criteria, depending on the type of food provided. There are some exceptions from registration for childminders in certain circumstances and this is based on guidance produced by the Food Standards Agency.

The legal requirements aim to ensure that safe food is produced and to reduce the risk of poisoning. There have been a number of high profile cases that have been linked to childcare settings. Knowledge and control of food allergies is also a critical consideration in the production and service of safe food.

A healthy, balanced and nutritious diet

 EYFS 3.45

This requirement outlines the importance of a healthy, balanced diet for all children. Menu planning is crucial to ensure all children's nutritional needs, specific requirements and preferences are incorporated. For more information on supporting children's health and self-care see 'Early years outcomes' (Ref. DFE-00167-2013). https://www.gov.uk/government/uploads/system/uploads/attachment_data/file/237249/Early_Years_Outcomes.pdf

Always check the latest nutritional guidelines for babies and young children when planning menus: http://www.food.gov.uk.

Ensure your menus include a good balance across the main food groups:

- starchy foods: breads, cereals, rice, pasta and noodles
- fruit and vegetables
- milk and dairy product, such as yoghurt and cheese
- proteins, including meat, fish, poultry, eggs, tofu and nuts
- fats and carbohydrates, including oils, margarine and sugars.

 Remember

Growing your own fruit and vegetables helps children understand about food origins, the fundamentals of organic gardening and taking care of plants. Children tend to be more enthusiastic about trying new foods they have grown themselves, such as strawberries, tomatoes and cress.

Special dietary requirements

 EYFS 3.45

It is essential to gather all information relevant to children's dietary needs prior to them starting at your setting. Do this in consultation with parents, carers and children.

Special dietary requirements to consider are:

- food allergies, such as nuts, gluten and cows' milk protein allergy (CMPA)
- food intolerance, such as to dairy products
- coeliac disease
- phenylketonuria (PKU)
- diabetes
- cultural requirements
- religious requirements
- vegetarian.

 Remember

Ensure all of your staff are aware of children's specific dietary needs. Think about how and where this information is displayed. Are children's photographs used to identify specific considerations? Remember to be respectful and sensitive to children's specific needs and not have information displayed in a public area.

Weaning

It is important to consider babies and toddlers when planning menus as some fruits and vegetables can be easily introduced as part of the weaning process. Weaning is a gradual process and needs to be done in consultation with parents and carers.

 Remember

Healthy eating food fact sheets can be found on The British Dietetic Association (BDA) website: http://www.bda.uk.com.

Supervision is extremely important when babies are weaning as finger foods such as slices of mango, melon and pear can pose choking hazards for children. Even toddlers can struggle with chunky food and choke easily. Always ensure staff sit with children at mealtimes.

The Ofsted newsletter in June 2011 highlighted the risk of young children choking on food and the importance of first aid training covering the skills required to help dislodge food from the throats of young children. It covered the preparation of food for young children, suggesting that food, such as a round sausage or banana, is cut lengthways rather than crossways to avoid creating a 'perfect plug' that children could choke on. For more information see http://www. ofsted.gov.uk/resources/early-years-june-2011.

Remember

Always check with parents and carers before trying new foods with children. Your local health visitor and dietician can offer training and good advice to staff and children's families regarding healthy eating. For more advice on weaning and healthy eating: http://www.nhs.uk/ Conditions/pregnancy-and-baby/Pages/solid-foods-weaning.aspx#close.

Mealtimes should be happy, sociable occasions – just as adults enjoy eating out; children need time and space to develop these skills.

Drinks

 EYFS 3.45

You must provide access to fresh drinking water for all children. Children can easily and quickly become dehydrated. They need to learn the importance of drinking water throughout the day and after physical exercise. You may need to consider how you will manage this with a mixed age group, as younger children may require support and supervision in accessing drinking water.

Remember

Ensure you have sufficient, suitable cups and beakers to encourage children to access water.

Suitable facilities for food preparation and competent staff

 EYFS 3.46

It is crucial to consider food hygiene in relation to food preparation. The kitchen area must be clean, suitable and contain equipment, in full working order, to enable the safe preparation of food. For example, a cooker, microwave, fridge, freezer and wash hand-basin will be needed.

Specific equipment may be required dependent on the needs of the children you are caring for. For example, in order to prepare milk feed for babies, you will require sterilising equipment, bottles and teats.

Remember

Read food labels and instructions carefully when preparing feeds for babies. Overdosing a baby on formula powder can cause dehydration, kidney and digestive problems for babies. Also, ensure the correct formula is given to the correct child. Giving a baby with cows' milk protein allergy (CMPA) a cows' milk feed by mistake could have very serious health consequences for that child.

Training

 EYFS 3.46

Any staff designated to prepare and handle food in a group setting must hold a valid food hygiene certificate. Ensure staff access approved food hygiene courses.

Remember

If you employ a part-time cook, you will need to train other staff in food hygiene as they may be required to prepare breakfasts or teas in the cook's absence.

Law

Ofsted guidance states notification must be made as soon as is reasonably practicable and in any event within 14 days.

Notifications regarding food poisoning

 EYFS 3.47 and CR 13

If you have two or more children become ill after eating at your setting, you must make appropriate notifications to the Health Protection Agency and Environmental Health in conjunction with Ofsted.

Childminders

The above guidance applies to childminders who also need to consider the following:

 EYFS 3.46

Consider the organisation of mealtimes and ensure you have sufficient equipment, such as high chairs, age/stage appropriate cutlery, cups and plates. It is important for childminders to encourage children to try different foods and tastes and make mealtimes a sociable, learning occasion. When caring for babies and toddlers, think about how you keep parents and carers informed about children's weaning progress.

For more information on food safety there is a useful leaflet at http://www.food.gov.uk called 'Food safety advice for childminders'.

Registration of a food business

➡ Regulation EC No. 178/2002 Chapter 1 Article 3(2)

A food business is defined in the European Community regulations as any undertaking, whether for profit or not and whether public or private, carrying out any of the activities related to any stage of production, processing and distribution of food.

➡ Regulation EC No. 852/2004 Chapter II Article 6(2)

The law requires a food business operator to register details of their food business with the local authority (your local Environmental Health Department of your local council) 28 days before starting a food business.

If you prepare, produce, handle or store food for your children in your setting, you need to complete this registration. Advice can be sought from your local Environmental Health Department. There is also advice on the Food Standards Agency's website at http://www.food.gov.uk.

You are likely to receive an initial inspection from an Environmental Health/Food Safety Officer on receipt of your registration. The officer will inspect to ensure that you are meeting your legal duties and risk rate the food business to determine how often a food hygiene and food standards inspection should take place.

Childminders

- Childminders who regularly prepare, handle and provide food for the children in their care were required to register as a food business. This means that your food business at your home required registration.
- However, the food provided by childminders can vary in terms of what is offered. The Food Standards Agency has produced guidance for childcarers in a domestic setting. It is available at www.food.gov.uk/business-industry/caterers/sfbb/sfbbchildminders/Cached.
- The guidance contains certain exemptions from registration for childminders. This depends on the type of food supplied to the children.
- The Food Standards Agency has completed a consultation in England on the requirement for certain childminders to register as a food business. This has led to a very recent change in requirements. From 1 January 2014 new childminders, operating their business in domestic premises, are no longer required to register separately as a food business. There is now a single registration process based on collaboration between Ofsted and the local authority. However your business may still be inspected for food safety by the local authority.

Providing safe food

➡ Regulation EC No. 178/2002 Chapter II Section 4 Article 14

Food business operators have a legal duty to produce food that is safe to eat. Food is considered to be unsafe if it is injurious to health or unfit for human consumption. This means that the food should not have an adverse effect on the consumer's health and it should not be contaminated. If the food business operator fails to meet this requirement they are committing an offence and can be prosecuted.

Know where your food comes from

➡️ Regulation EC No. 178/2002 Chapter II Section 4 Article 18

The law requires that the food business operator can identify who has supplied them with a food product. This is really important in the event of a problem with the food.

Ensure that your food business meets legal requirements

➡️ Regulation EC No. 852/2004 Chapter II Article 4(2) Annex II

In general terms these regulations detail the requirements of premises, practices and personnel to ensure safe food.

The regulations contain detailed requirements for:

- food premises generally
- food rooms where food is prepared, treated or processed
- movable or temporary food premises
- transportation of food
- food equipment
- food waste
- water supply
- personal hygiene
- preventing the contamination of foodstuffs
- wrapping and packaging
- heat treatment of certain products
- training of food handlers
- training of responsible persons.

The regulations stipulate general requirements to ensure that the structure of the premises is capable of being maintained, cleaned and/or disinfected and that it prevents access by pests, for example, rats and mice. Any food surfaces or equipment must also be capable of being cleaned and disinfected.

The regulations also specify where sinks may be required for the washing of food, for the cleaning and disinfection of equipment and utensils, and require that an adequate number of toilets and wash hand-basins are available.

The type of food and the food operation at settings will differ significantly. You may be preparing cooked meals, having cooked food delivered for service or be preparing snacks only. In this way the risk and the requirements for the business will differ.

When planning any food business seek advice from your local Environmental Health Department. They will be able to give you advice on how to comply with the law within your business. This may prevent costly errors.

Childminders

Your food operation takes place in a domestic setting and this will be taken into account. The area where food is prepared, stored and the toilet facilities may be subject to a routine food hygiene inspection by Environmental Health. An alternative enforcement strategy may be used instead of a visit, for example completion of a questionnaire.

Training

→ Regulation EC No. 852/2004 Chapter II Article 4(2) Annex II Chapter XII Requirement 1

The regulations recognise the importance of supervising, instructing and training food handlers in food hygiene so that they are competent in the tasks that they are required to do.

The regulations do not go as far as prescribing a formal training course or qualification. The type of training, instruction and supervision is dependent on the type of food offered, the volume and the risk.

In a small setting producing hot meals a level of training recommended for the food handler would be the Chartered Institute of Environmental Health's Level 2 award in food safety catering or an equivalent course.

For simpler food offerings such as snacks, instruction and supervision in the basic rules of food hygiene prior to starting work may be acceptable.

The Food Standards Agency has produced a document called 'Safer food, better business for caterers'. This document details the safe methods for producing, storing and serving food. It also provides a food safety management system, including a programme for staff training and recording training. The document is available free of charge from the FSA or it can be downloaded from http://www.food.gov.uk/business-industry/caterers/sfbb/.

Childminders

The Food Standards Agency has also produced a 'Safer food, better business pack for childminders'. This document takes into account that you are providing food using your own domestic kitchen. 'Safer food, better business for childminders' is available at http://www.food.gov.uk/business-industry/caterers/sfbb/.

 Law

Although the law relating to food hygiene training is not prescriptive, EYFS 3.46 does stipulate a specific standard for settings.

Food safety practices and procedures

Following good food safety practices is an important part of food safety management to prevent food poisoning and food borne illness.

→ Regulation EC No. 852/2004 Chapter II Article 5

The regulations require food business operators to put in place, implement and maintain a permanent procedure or procedures based on HACCP principles.

HACCP stands for hazard analysis, critical control point and is a management system based on risk assessment, looking at food safety hazards in your business. The ultimate aim of this technique is to ensure that the food you produce is safe to eat.

It requires a business to:

- Look at the food that is produced from the stages of purchasing the ingredients to the production and service of the finished product.
- Identify the food safety hazards. These are the points where the food could become contaminated with physical, chemical or biological contaminants that could make the food unsafe to eat.
- Identify critical control points – those steps in the process where if you do not control the hazard then it will not be controlled at any other point further on in the process. This could result in the production of unsafe food and this point is critical to food safety.
- Put controls in place at this point to eliminate or reduce the food hazard to an acceptable level.
- Check and monitor the controls at this stage to make sure that they are working and know what to do if things go wrong.
- Keep documentation and a simple record to demonstrate that you have done this.
- Review the HACCP document if there is a change in the product, process or any step.

A closer look at 'Safer food, better business'

The Food Standards Agency developed information packs to enable small businesses including childminders to comply with this requirement to develop and implement a food safety management system based on HACCP. They contain safe methods to ensure safe food production. These are based on some very essential rules about food hygiene that anyone preparing food should be aware of and which, if followed, reduce the risk of food poisoning and contamination.

The safe methods are:

- preventing cross-contamination
- cleaning
- chilling
- cooking.

There is also a management section to help you with training, cleaning schedules, start and end of business checks, proving your food practices are safe and a daily diary for records.

There is guidance on how to use the pack. Packs and diary sheet refills are available free of charge.

Scotland has developed its own food safety management system called 'CookSafe'. This is available at http://www.food.gov.uk/scotland/safetyhygienescot/cooksafe/. 'Safe Catering' is the system in Northern Ireland.

Training in HACCP principles

➡️ Regulation EC No. 852/2004 Chapter II Article 4(2) Annex II Chapter XII Requirement 2

The regulations also require that those who are responsible for developing and maintaining the HACCP system have received training in HACCP principles to enable them to do their job. There are training courses available.

There is a DVD that accompanies the 'Safer food, better business' packs, which tells you how to use it and how to apply it in your business. Some local authorities and private training organisations provide training and coaching on 'Safer food, better business'.

Remember

'Safer food, better business' is not suitable for every business, particularly if your food operation is complicated. You can get advice on food safety management systems such as HACCP from your local Environmental Health Department. They can assist you in deciding what is the right system for your business.

Essentials of food hygiene

The childcare sector provides food for very young children. This group is classed as 'vulnerable' because they are susceptible to food poisoning and food borne illness as their immune systems are still developing.

There are some very essential rules about food hygiene that anyone preparing food should be aware of which, if followed, reduces the risk of food poisoning and contamination occurring:

- keep food safe by preventing cross-contamination
- keep food safe by practising good personal hygiene
- cook food thoroughly and keep certain types of food at safe temperatures.

Guidance on preventing cross-contamination, good personal hygiene practice and temperature control can be found in the 'safe methods' in the 'Safer food, better business' and 'CookSafe' packs.

Further advice is also available in the Food Standards Agency's leaflet 'Food hygiene – a guide for businesses' available at http//:www.food.gov.uk.

> **Remember**
>
> Regular hand washing is an essential part of good personal hygiene and it important that hands are washed frequently and thoroughly.
>
> Alcohol gels are no substitute for washing hands with warm water and liquid soap and drying the hands thoroughly with a disposable paper towel. Alcohol gels may be applied after hand washing has taken place.

Notification of certain conditions and illnesses by food handlers

⟶ Regulation EC No. 852/2004 Chapter II Article 4(2) Annex II Chapter VIII Requirement 2

Staff are responsible for notifying the food business operator immediately if they are suffering from certain conditions or illnesses that could result in contamination of food, for example, infected wounds, sores, diarrhoea and vomiting. The purpose of the notification is to allow you to deal with the matter.

Providers need to have a robust policy on staff illness and their staff must be aware of this policy and follow it.

Based on guidance by the Health Protection Agency (HPA), any person suffering from diarrhoea and/or vomiting should be excluded from the premises for a period of 48 hours after their symptoms have ceased. This is because even when symptoms have stopped the person can still be infectious and transfer the infection to others.

Providers may need to consider asking for medical clearance via the GP through the submission of faecal specimens, based on the persistence of the symptoms and/or subsequent diagnosis of the illness for example, e.coli 0157, typhoid, paratyphoid and hepatitis A or illness following holiday travel.

In such cases where a diagnosis of a case of food poisoning or a food borne illness takes place, the GP should notify the HPA, and environmental health staff will become involved and will investigate and manage the screening of the case.

You need to apply the same rules to your other staff and children as cases of gastroenteritis, food poisoning and food borne illness can spread rapidly in settings.

You can obtain advice from the local Environmental Health Department on dealing with isolated cases of food poisoning, food borne illness or other infectious diseases.

Outbreaks of an infectious disease and/or gastroenteritis

An outbreak is defined as 'two or more linked cases of the same disease or when the observed number of cases unaccountably exceeds the expected number'.

http://food.gov.uk/multimedia/pdfs/outbreakmanaagement.pdf.

Infection from case to case can spread rapidly if good personal and strict environmental controls are not put in place.

Bacteria and viruses can be passed on from person to person in many ways, through direct contact, aerosols, droplets, faecal oral route, and body fluids.

You should have a robust plan for dealing with outbreaks. You also need to apply strict infection control procedures. The plan and the procedures should be communicated and understood by staff.

The Health Protection Agency has produced guidance on infection control entitled 'Guidance on Infection Control in Schools and other Child Care Settings'. This can be downloaded from their website at http:/www.hpa.org.uk.

There is also a 'Norovirus Toolkit' entitled 'A set of resources for staff in schools and nurseries' available at http:/www.hpa.org.uk.

It is very important that if you suspect that there is an outbreak at or connected to your setting that you notify the Infection Control Team in Environmental Health and the Infection Control Nurse in your regional Public Health Unit.

 Remember

From 1 April 2013 the HPA was replaced by Public Health England, Public Health Scotland, Public Health Wales and the Public Health Agency covering Northern Ireland

Food allergies

Food allergies can be life threatening so it is very important that there are robust procedures in place to enable:

- the identification of children with allergies, through discussion with parents and carers
- the identification of the nature of the allergy
- effective communication to staff
- control of foods including the checking of ingredients, labels on food and labelling food clearly in house
- prevention of contamination through restriction policies, proper hand washing techniques and thorough cleaning of work surfaces and equipment prior to food preparation
- recognising symptoms of an allergic reaction
- knowing what to do.

There is detailed information on food allergies and on the common types of food that people can be allergic to in the 'Safer food, better business' and 'CookSafe' packs. Further information about food allergies can be found at http://www.food.gov.uk/policy-advice/allergyintol/.

 Remember

Your first aider should know what to do in the event of a casualty affected by an allergy.

Glossary of abbreviations

ACM	Asbestos containing materials
ACOP	Approved Code of Practice
BSEN	British Standard European Norm
COSHH	Control of Substances Hazardous to Health Regulations 2002 (as amended)
CMPA	Cows' Milk Protein Allergy
CPD	Continuing Professional Development
CR	Childcare Register
CWDC	Children's Workforce Development Council
DfE	Department for Education
DPA	Data Protection Act
DSE	Display screen equipment
EFAW	Emergency First Aid At Work
EYE	Early Years Educator
EYFS	Early Years Foundation Stage
EYP	Early Years Professional
EYPS	Early Years Professional Status
EYT	Early Years Teacher
EYR	Early Years Register
FAW	First Aid At Work
GP	General Practitioner
HACCP	Hazard Analysis, Critical Control Point
HSE	Health and Safety Executive
HSWA	Health and Safety at Work Etc. Act 1974
IEP	Individual Education Plan
LA	Local Authority
LADO	Local Authority Designated Officer
LSCB	Local Safeguarding Children Board
MAC	Manual handling assessment chart
NNEB	National Nursery Examination Board
Ofsted	Office for Standards in Education
OT	Occupational Therapist
PAT	Portable appliance testing
PGCE	Postgraduate Certificate in Education
PPC	Personal protective clothing
PPE	Personal protective equipment
PUWER	Provision and Use of Work Equipment Regulations 1998
QTS	Qualified Teacher Status
RIDDOR	Reporting of Injuries, Diseases and Dangerous Occurrences Regulations 2013
ROSPA	Royal Society for the Prevention of Accidents
SaLT	Speech and Language Therapist
SEND	Special Educational Needs and Disabilities
SCR	Serious Case Review
TMV	Thermostatic mixing valve

Bibliography

This book contains public sector information licensed under the Open Government Licence vs.http://www.nationalarchives.gov.uk/doc/open-government-licence/.

This includes public sector information published by the Health and Safety Executive and licensed under the Open Government Licence v1.0.

British Dietetic Association (BDA). http://www.bda.uk.com (accessed 23 July 2012).

Childcare Act 2006. http://www.education.gov.uk/childrenandyoungpeople/earlylearningandchildcare/delivery/a0071032/childcare-act-2006 (accessed 23 July 2012).

Childcare Act 2006. www.opsi.gov.uk/ACTS/acts2006/ukpga_20060021_en_1 (accessed 29 July 2012).

Children and Families Bill 2013 (October 2013). http://www.education.gov.uk/a00221161 (accessed 27 September 2013).

Children and Families Bill 2013. Childminder agencies. https://www.gov.uk/government/policies/improving-the-quality-and-range-of-education-and-childcare-from-birth-to-5-years/supporting-pages/childminder-agencies (accessed 22 October 2013).

The Disclosure and Barring Service (DBS) 'Helping employers make safer recruiting decisions' (DBS 2013). https://www.gov.uk/government/policies/helping-employers-make-safer-recruiting-decisions (accessed 27 September 2013).

Department for Business, Innovation and Skills (2011) 'The Toys (Safety) Regulations 2011. Guidelines on the appointment of UK notified bodies', Reference URN 11/1263.

Department for Children, Schools and Families (2008) *Analysing child deaths and serious injury through abuse and neglect: what can we learn?* ISBN 978 1 84775 096 9. Nottingham: DCSF.

Department for Children, Schools and Families (2010) 'Working Together to Safeguard Children', ref: 00305-2010DOM-EN. Nottingham. DCSF. https://www.education.gov.uk/publications/standard/publicationDetail/Page1/DCSF-00305-2010 (accessed 28 July 2012).

Department for Children, Schools and Families (2010) 'A guide to inter-agency working to safeguard and promote the welfare of children'. Nottingham: DCSF.

Department for Communities and Local Government. http://www.communities.gov.uk/fire/firesafety/firesafetylaw/ (accessed 26 July 2012).

Department of Education (2012) 'Early years outcomes'. https://www.gov.uk/government/uploads/system/uploads/attachment_data/file/237249/Early_Years_Outcomes.pdf (accessed 27 September 2013).

Department of Education (2012) 'Graduate leaders in Early Years: EYPS explained'. http://www.education.gov.uk/childrenandyoungpeople/earlylearningandchildcare/delivery/b00201345/graduate-leaders/eyps (accessed 18 July 2012).

Department of Education (2012) *Support and aspiration: A new approach to special educational needs and disability. Progress and next steps*, ISBN 978-1-78105-072-9. London: TSO.

Department for Education. 'Statutory Framework for the Early Years Foundation Stage'. http://www.education.gov.uk/schools/teachingandlearning/curriculum/a0068102/early-years-foundation-stage-eyfs (accessed 23 July 2012).

Department of Education (2013) 'Graduate leaders/early years teachers'. http://www.education.gov.uk/childrenandyoungpeople/earlylearningandchildcare/h00201345/graduate-leaders/early-years-teachers (accessed 22 October 2013).

Department of Education (2013) 'Early years teachers' standards'. https://www.gov.uk/government/publications/early-years-teachers-standards (accessed 22 October 2013).

Department for Education (2013) 'Working Together to Safeguard Children. A guide to inter-agency working to safeguard and promote the welfare of children' (March 2013). http://www.education.gov.uk/aboutdfe/statutory/g00213160/working-together-to-safeguard-children (accessed 27 September 2013).

Department for Work and Pensions (2011) *The Government response to the Löfstedt Report*, ISBN 978-1-84947-915-8. London.

Drug Awareness. http://www.direct.gov.uk/en/Parents/Yourchildshealthandsafety/WorriedAbout/DG_10026450.

Early Years Foundation Stage (Welfare Requirements) Regulations 2007. www.opsi.gov.uk/si/si2007/uksi_20071771_en_1.

EYFS progress check at age two. https://www.education.gov.uk/publications/.../NCB-00087-2012 (accessed 23 July 2012).

Food Hygiene (England) Regulations 2006 (as amended). TSO. SI 2006 No. 14.

Food Standards Agency (2008) 'Management of outbreaks of foodborne illness in England and Wales'. http://www.food.gov.uk/multimedia/pdfs/outbreakmanagement/pdf (accessed 23 July 2012).

Food Standards Agency 'Safer food better business for childminders' (2009). http://www.food.gov.uk/business-industry/caterers/sfbb/sfbbchildminders/ (accessed 18 July 2012).

Food Standards Agency Open Board – 22 May 2012 'Childminders and Community Halls'. Report by Alison Gleadle, Director Food Safety Group.

General Food Regulations 2004 (as amended). TSO. SI 2004 No. 3279.

Health Protection Agency North West 'Infection Prevention and Communicable Disease Control Guidance for Early Years and School Settings' (2011) (version two). http://www.hpa.org.uk/webc/HPAwebFile/HPAweb_C/1194947365864 (accessed 18 July 2012).

Health and Safety Commission (HSC) 'Management of Health and Safety at Work Regulations 1999 Approved Code of Practice & guidance' series code L21, (2000) (second edition) HSE Books. http://www.hse.gov.uk/pubns/books/l21.htm (accessed 18 July 2012).

HSC 'Safe use of work equipment Provision and use of Work Equipment Regulations 1998 Approved Code of Practice and guidance', series code L22 (2008) (third edition) HSE Books. http://books.hse.gov.uk/hse/public/saleproduct.jsf?catalogueCode=9780717662951 (accessed 18 July 2012).

Health and Safety Executive/Local Authorities Enforcement Liaison Committee (HELA) Local Authority Circular LAC Number: 22/19 'Formal cautions. HSE Guidance', (Revised September 2003). http://www.hse.gov.uk/lau/lacs/22-19.htm (accessed 18 July 2012).

Health and Safety Executive (HSE) 'Legionnaires' disease The control of legionella bacteria in water systems Approved Code of Practice and guidance', series code L8 (2000) (third edition) HSE Books. http://www.hse.gov.uk/pubns/priced/l8.pdf (accessed 18 July 2012).

HSE 'Health and safety in care homes', series code HSG220 (2001) (first edition) HSE Books. http://books.hse.gov.uk/hse/public/saleproduct.jsf?catalogueCode=9780717620821 (accessed 18 July 2012).

HSE 'Manual Handling. Manual Handling Operations Regulations 1992 (as amended) Guidance on Regulations', series code L23 (2004) (third edition) HSE Books. http://books.hse.gov.uk/hse/public/saleproduct.jsf?catalogueCode=9780717628230 (accessed 18 July 2012).

HSE 'Workplace health, safety and welfare. Workplace (Health, Safety and Welfare) Regulations 1992 Approved Code of Practice', series code L24 (2004) (twelfth edition) HSE Books. http://www.hse.gov.uk/pubns/books/l24.htm (accessed 8 October 2013).

HSE 'Control of substances hazardous to health The Control of Substances Hazardous to Health Regulations 2002 (as amended) Approved Code of Practice and guidance', series code L5 (2005) (fifth edition) HSE Books. http://books.hse.gov.uk/hse/public/saleproduct.jsf?catalogueCode=9780717629817 (accessed 18 July 2012).

HSE 'Personal protective equipment at work Personal Protective Equipment at Work Regulations 1992 (as amended) Guidance on Regulations', series code L25 (2005) (second edition) HSE Books. (http://books.hse.gov.uk/hse/public/saleproduct.jsf?catalogueCode=9780717661398 (accessed 18 July 2012).

HSE 'The management of asbestos in non-domestic premises Regulation 4 of the Control of Asbestos at Work Regulations 2006. Approved Code of Practice and guidance', series guide L127 (2006) (second edition) HSE Books. http://www.hse.gov.uk/pubns/priced/l127.pdf (accessed 18 July 2012).

HSE 'The Health and Safety (First-Aid) Regulations 1981 Approved Code of Practice and guidance', series code L74 (2009) (second edition) HSE Books. http://books.hse.gov.uk/hse/public/saleproduct. jsf?catalogueCode=9780717662609 (accessed 18 July 2012).

HSE 'Consulting employees on health and safety A brief guide to the law', leaflet INDG 232 (2011) (rev1). http://www.hse.gov.uk/pubns/indg232.pdf (accessed 18 July 2012).

HSE 'Five Steps to Risk Assessment', leaflet INDG163 (2011) (rev3). http://www.hse.gov.uk/pubns/indg163. pdf (accessed 18 July 2012).

HSE 'Managing health and safety. Five Steps to Success', leaflet INDG 275 (2011). http://www.hse.gov.uk/ pubns/indg275.pdf (accessed 18 July 2012).

HSE 'Safety in the installation and use of gas systems and appliances Gas Safety (Installation and Use) Regulations 1998 Approved Code of Practice and guidance', series code L56 (2011) (third edition) HSE Books. http://www.hse.gov.uk/pubns/priced/l56.pdf (accessed 18 July 2012).

HSE 'School trips and outdoor learning activities. Tackling the health and safety myths', leaflet (2011). http:// www.hse.gov.uk/services/education/school-trips.pdf (accessed 18 July 2012).

HSE 'A guide to the Reporting of Injuries, Diseases and Dangerous Occurrences Regulations 1995', series code L73 (2012) (fourth edition) HSE Books. http://www.hse.gov.uk/pubns/books/l73.htm (accessed 18 July 2012).

HSE 'Electrical safety and you. A brief guide', leaflet INDG231 (2012) (rev1). http://www.hse.gov.uk/pubns/ indg231.pdf (accessed 18 July 2012).

HSE 'Maintaining portable electric equipment in low-risk environments', leaflet INDG236 (2012) (rev2). http://www.hse.gov.uk/pubns/indg236.pdf (accessed 18 July 2012).

HSE 'Managing asbestos in buildings: A brief guide', leaflet INDG223 (2012)(rev5). http://www.hse.gov.uk/ pubns/indg223.pdf (accessed 18 July 2012).

HSE 'First aid at work. The Health and Safety (First-Aid) Regulations 1981. Guidance on Regulation' series code L74 (2013) (third edition) HSE Books. http://www.hse.gov.uk/pubns/books/l74.htm (accessed 8 October 2013).

HSE 'National Local Authority Enforcement Code Health and Safety at Work England, Scotland & Wales' (2013). http://www.hse.gov.uk/lau/national-la-code.pdf (accessed 3 June 2013).

HSE 'Reporting accidents and incidents at work. A brief guide to the Reporting of Injuries, Diseases and Dangerous Occurrences Regulations 2013 (RIDDOR)', leaflet INDG453 (rev1) (2013). http://www.hse.gov. uk/pubns/indg453-rev1.pdf (accessed 8 October 2013).

HSE Local Authority Unit 'Health and Safety (Enforcing Authority) Regulations 1998: A–Z guide to allocation', OC 124/11 (2011) (Rev 3 17/11/2011 (htm). http://www.hse.gov.uk/foi/internalops/fod/oc/100-199/124-11.htm (accessed 18 July 2012).

Health and Safety at Work Etc. Act 1974. TSO.

Health and Safety (Enforcing Authority) Regulations 1998. TSO. SI 1998 No. 494.

Health and Safety (First Aid) Regulations 1981. TSO. SI 1981 No. 917.

Her Majesty's Government (2006) *Fire safety risk assessment guide educational establishments*. ISBN: 978 1 85112 819 8. http://www.ommunities.gov.uk/fire/firesafety/firesafetylaw/ (accessed 26 July 2012).

Home safety; Directgov. http://www.direct.gov.uk/en/homeandcommunity/inyourhome/ keepingsafeathome/dg_10029724 (accessed 23 July 2012).

Heuristic play. http://www.educationscotland.gov.uk/resources/h/genericresource_tcm4242264.asp (accessed 29 July 2012).

Independent Safeguarding Authority. http://www.isa.homeoffice.gov.uk/default.aspx (accessed 30 July 2012).

Limitation Act 1980; 1980 Chapter 58; section 11; Special time limit for actions in respect of personal injuries. http://www.legislation.gov.uk/ukpga/1980/58/contents (accessed 18 July 2012).

Literacy Trust. http://www.literacytrust.org.uk/early_years (accessed 30 July 2012).

Lock, R. (2013) 'Coventry Safeguarding Children Board. Serious case review; Daniel Pelka'. September 2013. http://www.coventrylscb.org.uk/files/SCR/FINAL%20Overview%20Report%20%20DP%20 130913%20Publication%20version.pdf (accessed 22 October 2013).

Löfstedt, Professor Ragnar E (November 2011) *Reclaiming health and safety for all: An independent review of health and safety legislation.* ISBN: 9780101821926.

The Lord Laming (2009) 'The Protection of Children in England: A Progress Report'. London: TSO. https://www.education.gov.uk/publications/.../HC-330.pdf (accessed 28 July 2012).

Lundberg, B. (2013) 'Birmingham Safeguarding Children Board. Serious case review; Keanu Williams'. September 2013. http://www.lscbbirmingham.org.uk/images/stories/downloads/executive-summaries/ Case_25__Final_Overview_Report_02.10.13.pdf (accessed 22 October 2013).

NHS choice. http://www.nhs.uk/Livewell/Childrenssleep/Pages/babysleeptips.aspx (accessed 23 July 2012).

Nutbrown Review (2012) 'Foundations for quality. The independent review of early education and childcare qualifications. Final Report', Cheshire. http://www.education.gov.uk/nutbrownreview (accessed 28 July 2012).

Ofsted. http://www.ofsted.gov.uk/resources/factsheet-childcare-registration-and-inspection-of-providers-who-hold-exemptions-learning-and-develo (accessed 25 July 2012). http://www.ofsted.gov.uk/resources/ compliance-investigation-and-enforcement-handbook (accessed 29 July 2012). http://www.ofsted.gov.uk/ resources/factsheet-childcare-serious-accidents-injuries-and-deaths-registered-providers-must-notify-ofsted-an (accessed 29 July 2012).

Ofsted (2010) 'Safeguarding policy and procedures', No. 100183. Manchester: Ofsted. http://www.ofsted. gov.uk/resources/ofsted-safeguarding-policy-and-procedures. (accessed 28 July 2012).

Ofsted (2010) 'The special educational needs and disability review. Age group: 0–9', Reference no: 090221. Manchester: Ofsted. http://www.ofsted.gov.uk/resources/special-educational-needs-and-disability-review (accessed 28 July 2012).

Ofsted (2011) 'Information for parents and carers using childcare services,' No. 080025. http://www.ico.gov. uk (accessed 28 July 2012).

Ofsted (2011) 'Registration and suitability handbook. Guidance for inspectors and regulatory decision-makers on the registration and continued registration of those on the Early Years and Childcare Registers', No. 100165. Manchester: Ofsted. http://www.ofsted.gov.uk/resources/registration-and-suitability-handbook (accessed 28 July 2012).

Ofsted (2012) 'Applying to waive disqualification', No. 080054. Manchester: Ofsted. http://www.ofsted. gov.uk/resources/applying-waive-disqualification (accessed 28 July 2012).

Ofsted (2012) 'Are you ready for your inspection? A guide to inspections of provision on Ofsted's Childcare and Early Years Registers'. http:// www.ofsted.gov.uk/resources/are-you-ready-for-your-inspection-guide-inspections-of-provision-ofsteds-childcare-and-early-years-r (accessed 4 September 2012).

Ofsted (2012) 'Conducting early years inspections'. http://www.ofsted.gov.uk/resources/conducting-early-years-inspections (accessed 22 October 2013).

Ofsted (2012) 'Evaluation schedule for inspections of registered early years provision'. http://www.ofsted. gov.uk/resources/evaluation-schedule-for-inspections-of-registered-early-years-provision (accessed 4 September 2012).

Ofsted (2012) 'Framework for the regulation of provision on the Early Years Register'. http://www.ofsted. gov.uk/resources/framework-for-regulation-of-provision-early-years-register (accessed 22 October 2013).

Ofsted (2013) 'Compliance, investigation and enforcement handbook: childminding and childcare'. http://www.ofsted.gov.uk/resources/compliance-investigation-and-enforcement-handbook-childminding-and-childcare (accessed 22 October 2013).

Ofsted (2013) 'Conducting priority and brought forward inspections following risk assessment' (July 2013). http://www.ofsted.gov.uk/resources/conducting-priority-and-brought-forward-inspections-following-risk-assessment (accessed 22 October 2013).

Ofsted (2013) 'Evaluation schedule for inspections of registered early years provision' (October 2013). http://www.ofsted.gov.uk/resources/evaluation-schedule-for-inspections-of-registered-early-years-provision (accessed 22 October 2013).

Ofsted: Early Years Newsletters. http://www.ofsted.gov.uk/resources/early-years-june-2011 (accessed 29 July 2012).

Ofsted: Early Years Register (2010) 'Preparing for your registration visit April 2010', reference no: 080021. Manchester: Ofsted. http://www.ofsted.gov.uk/resources/childcare-registration-form-early-years-register-preparing-for-your-registration-visit (accessed 29 July 2012).

Ofsted Factsheet: 'Applying to waive disqualification'. http://www.ofsted.gov.uk/resources/applying-waive-disqualification (accessed 22 October 2013).

Ofsted Factsheet: 'Childminders using assistants'. http://www.ofsted.gov.uk/resources/factsheet-childcare-childminders-using-assistants (accessed 29 July 2012).

Ofsted Factsheet: 'Common core skills and knowledge'. http://www.ofsted.gov.uk/resources/factsheet-childcare-common-core-skills-and-knowledge (accessed 29 July 2012).

Ofsted Factsheet: 'Disclosure and Barring Service (DBS) checks for those providers who register with Ofsted'. http://www.ofsted.gov.uk/resources/factsheet-childcare-disclosure-and-barring-service-dbs-checks-for-those-providers-who-register-ofste (accessed 27 September 2013).

Ofsted Factsheet: 'Giving medication to children in registered childcare'. http://www.ofsted.gov.uk/resources/factsheet-childcare-giving-medication-children-registered-childcare (accessed 27 September 2013).

Ofsted Factsheet: 'Requirements for the Childcare Register: childcare providers on non-domestic or domestic premises'. http://www.ofsted.gov.uk/resources/factsheet-childcare-requirements-for-childcare-register-childminders-and-home-childcarers (accessed 22 October 2013).

Ofsted Factsheet: 'Requirements for the Childcare Register: childminders and home childcarers'. http://www.ofsted.gov.uk/resources/factsheet-childcare-requirements-for-childcare-register-childminders-and-home-childcarers (accessed 29 July 2012).

Ofsted Factsheet: 'Requirements for written documents: childminders delivering the Early Years Foundation Stage (EYFS)'. http://www.ofsted.gov.uk/resources/factsheet-childcare-requirements-for-written-documents-childminders-delivering-early-years-foundation (accessed 29 July 2012).

Ofsted Factsheet: 'The numbers and ages of children that providers on the Early Years and Childcare Registers may care for'. http://www.ofsted.gov.uk/resources/factsheet-childcare-numbers-and-ages-of-children-providers-early-years-and-childcare-registers-may-c (accessed 22 October 2013).

Ofsted Factsheet: 'The requirements of the Early Years Register'. http://www.ofsted.gov.uk/resources/factsheet-childcare-requirements-of-early-years-register (accessed 29 July 2012).

Ofsted Factsheet: 'Trigger for inspections'. http://www.ofsted.gov.uk/resources/factsheet-childcare-triggers-for-inspections-of-those-early-years-and-childcare-registers (accessed 22 October 2013).

Ofsted Factsheet: 'Requirements for risk assessment'. (Ref 120334; November 2012) which includes outings. http://www.ofsted.gov.uk/resources/factsheet-childcare-requirements-for-risk-assessments (accessed 22 October 2013).

Ofsted Factsheet: 'Records, policies and notification requirements of the Early Years Register' January 2013. http://www.ofsted.gov.uk/resources/factsheet-childcare-records-policies-and-notification-requirements-of-early-years-register (accessed 27 September 2013).

Plymouth Safeguarding Children Board (2010) 'Overview Report Executive Summary in respect of Nursery Z. Final Executive Summary 2'. www.plymouth.gov.uk/serious_case_review_nursery_z.pdf (accessed 28 July 2012).

Queen's Printer and Controller of HMSO (March 2009) 'The Public Inquiry into the September 2005 Outbreak of E.coli O157 in South Wales'. London.

Regulation EC No. 178/2002 of the European Parliament and of the council of 28 January 2002 laying down the general principles and requirements of food law, establishing the European Food Safety Authority and laying down procedures in matters of food safety (pdf). Available at http://eur-lex.europa.eu/LexUriServ/LexUriServ.do?uri=OJ:L:2002:031:0001:0024:EN:PDF (accessed 18 July 2012).

Regulation EC No. 852/2004 of the European Parliament and of the council of 29 April 2004 on the hygiene of foodstuffs (pdf). Available at http://eur-lex.europa.eu/LexUriServ/LexUriServ.do?uri=OJ:L:2004:226:0003:0021:EN:PDF (accessed 18 July 2012).

Royal Society for the Prevention of Accidents (ROSPA). http://www.rospa.com/roadsafety/adviceandinformation/minibussafety/loading-safety.aspx (accessed 25 July 2012). http://www.rospa.com/leisuresafety/playsafety/ (accessed 26 July 2012).

Sun safety. http://www.sunsafenurseries.co.uk/ (accessed 30 July 2012).

The Play Company and Wickstead Leisure Limited (2008) 'An Essential Guide to BS EN 1176 and BS EN 1177 Children's Playground Equipment & Surfacing: updated for 2008'.

The Safeguarding Vulnerable Groups, part 5. https://www.gov.uk/government/publications/fact-sheet-safeguarding-of-vulnerable-groups-criminal-records-part-5 (accessed 27 September 2013).

The Control of Asbestos Regulations 2012. TSO. SI 2012 No. 632.

The Control of Substances Hazardous to Health Regulations 2002 (as amended). TSO. SI. 2002 No. 2677.

The Electricity at Work Regulations 1989. TSO. SI 1989 No. 365.

The Equality Act 2010 (Disability) Regulations 2010. TSO. SI 2010 No. 2128. Available at http://www.legislation.gov.uk/uksi/2010/2128/schedule/made (accessed 18 July 2012).

The Gas Safety (Installation and Use) Regulations 1998. TSO. SI 1998 No. 2451.

The Health & Safety (Consultation with Employees) Regulations 1996 (as amended). TSO. SI 1996 No. 1513.

The Health and Safety Information for Employees Regulations 1989 (as amended). TSO. SI 1989 No. 682.

The Management of Health and Safety at Work Regulations 1999. TSO. SI 1999 No. 3242.

The Manual Handling Operations Regulations 1992 (as amended). TSO. SI 1992 No. 2793.

The Personal Protective Equipment Regulations 1992 (as amended). TSO. SI 1992 No. 2966.

The Provision and Use of Work Equipment Regulations 1998. TSO. SI 1998 No. 2306.

The Regulatory Reform (Fire Safety) Order 2005. TSO.

The Reporting of Injuries, Accidents and Dangerous Occurrences Regulations 1995 (as amended). TSO. SI 1995 No. 3163.

The Reporting of Injuries, Diseases and Dangerous Occurrences Regulations 2013. TSO. SI 2013 No. 1471.

The Toys (Safety) Regulations 2011. TSO. SI 2011 No. 1881. http://www.legislation.gov.uk/uksi/2011/1881/made (accessed 18 July 2012).

The Workplace (Health, Safety and Welfare) Regulations 1992. TSO. SI 1992 No. 3004.

Whistleblower advice http://www.ofsted.gov.uk/contact-us/whistleblower-hotline (accessed 28 July 2012). http://www.pcaw.org.uk/ (accessed 28 July 2012).

Wonnacott, J. (2013) 'Serious case review case No. 2010–11/3'. http://www.lscbbirmingham.org.uk/images/stories/downloads/executive-summaries/Published_Overview_Report.pdf (accessed 22 October 2013).

Useful links

British Dietetic Association (BDA)
Healthy eating food fact sheets available at http://www.bda.uk.com (accessed 23 July 2012).

The Childcare Act 2006. http://www.education.gov.uk/childrenandyoungpeople/
earlylearningandchildcare/delivery/a0071032/childcare-act-2006 (accessed 23 July 2012).

The Childcare Act 2006.
www.opsi.gov.uk/ACTS/acts2006/ukpga_20060021_en_1 (accessed 29 July 2012).

Children and Families Bill 2013. Childminder agencies.
https://www.gov.uk/government/policies/improving-the-quality-and-range-of-education-and-childcare-
from-birth-to-5-years/supporting-pages/childminder-agencies (accessed 22 October 2013).

Department for Communities and Local Government
http://www.communities.gov.uk/fire/firesafety/firesafetylaw/ (accessed 26 July 2012).

Department for Children, Schools and Families (2008) 'Analysing child deaths and serious injury through
abuse and neglect: what can we learn?' ISBN 978 1 84775 096 9. Nottingham: DCSF.

Department for Children, Schools and Families (2010) 'A guide to inter-agency working to safeguard and
promote the welfare of children'. Nottingham: DCSF.

Department of Education (2012) 'Early years outcomes'.
https://www.gov.uk/government/uploads/system/uploads/attachment_data/file/237249/Early_Years_
Outcomes.pdf (accessed 27 September 2013).

Department of Education (2013) 'Graduate leaders/early years teachers'. http://www.education.gov.uk/
childrenandyoungpeople/earlylearningandchildcare/h00201345/graduate-leaders/early-years-teachers
(accessed 22 October 2013).

Department of Education (2013) 'Early years teachers' standards'.
https://www.gov.uk/government/publications/early-years-teachers-standards (accessed 22 October 2013).

Department of Education (2013) 'Improving the quality and range of education and childcare from birth to
5 years'. https://www.gov.uk/government/policies/improving-the-quality-and-range-of-education-and-
childcare-from-birth-to-5-years (accessed 22 October 2013).

Department for Education
http://www.education.gov.uk/ (accessed 26 July 2012).
'Statutory Framework for the Early Years Foundation Stage' at http://www.education.gov.uk/schools/
teachingandlearning/curriculum/a0068102/early-years-foundation-stage-eyfs (accessed 23 July 2012).

Department for Education (2013) 'Working together to safeguard children'.
http://www.education.gov.uk/aboutdfe/statutory/g00213160/working-together-to-safeguard-children
(accessed 27 September 2013).

The Disclosure and Barring Service (DBS)
https://www.gov.uk/government/organisations/disclosure-and-barring-service/about (accessed 27
September 2013).

The Disclosure and Barring Service (DBS) 'Helping employers make safer recruiting decisions' (DBS 2013)
https://www.gov.uk/government/policies/helping-employers-make-safer-recruiting-decisions (accessed 27
September 2013).

Drug Awareness
http://www.direct.gov.uk/en/Parents/Yourchildshealthandsafety/WorriedAbout/DG_10026450 (accessed
23 July 2012).

Early Years Foundation Stage (Welfare Requirements) Regulations 2007
www.opsi.gov.uk/si/si2007/uksi_20071771_en_1. (accessed 23 July 2012).

The EYFS progress check at age two
https://www.education.gov.uk/publications/.../NCB-00087-2012 (accessed 23 July 2012).

Education Scotland
http://www.educationscotland.gov.uk/resources/h/genericresource_tcm4242264.asp (accessed 23 July 2012).

Food Standards Agency. 'Allergies'.
http://www.food.gov.uk/policy-advice/allergyintol/ (accessed 23 July 2012).

Food Standards Agency. 'Hygiene guidance booklet'.
http://www.food.gov.uk/multimedia/pdfs/publication/hygieneguidebooklet.pdf (accessed 10 September 2012).

Food Standards Agency.
'Safer Food Better Business for Caterers' available from http://www.food.gov.uk/business-industry/caterers/sfbb/ (accessed 23 July 2012).

Food Standards Agency.
'Safer Food Better Business for Childminders' available from http://www.food.gov.uk/business-industry/caterers/sfbb/ (accessed 23 July 2012).

Foundation Years
http://www.foundationyears.org.uk (accessed 23 July 2012).

4Children
http://www.4children.org.uk/Home
(accessed 3 March 2014)

Home safety
Directgov website http://www.direct.gov.uk (accessed 23 July 2012).
http://www.direct.gov.uk/en/homeandcommunity/inyourhome/keepingsafeathome/dg_10029724 (accessed 23 July 2012).

Health and Safety Executive (HSE)
http://www.hse.gov.uk (accessed 23 July 2012).
http://www.hse.gov.uk/asbestos/regulations.htm (accessed 26 July 2012).
http://www.hse.gov.uk/coshh/ (accessed 27 July 2012).
http://www.hse.gov.uk/consult/condocs/cd241.htm (accessed 14 October 2013).
http://www.hse.gov.uk/contact/faqs/policy.htm (accessed 26 July 2012).
http://www.hse.gov.uk/msd/dse/ (accessed 26 July 2012).
http://www.hse.gov.uk/firstaid/whats-new/approval-training-providers-qualifications-first-aid-lofstedt.htm?eban=rss-first-aid-at-work (accessed 25 July 2012).
http://www.hse.gov.uk/firstaid/approved-training.htm (accessed 25 July 2012).
http://www.hse.gov.uk/gas/domestic/index.htm (accessed 27 July 2012).
http://www.hse.gov.uk/gas/domestic/newschemecontract.htm (accessed 3 June 2013).
http://www.hse.gov.uk/lau/publications/la-enforcement-code.htm?ebul=hsegen&cr=2/3-june-13 (accessed 3 June 2013).
http://www.hse.gov.uk/legionnaires/index.htm (accessed 26 July 2012).
http://www.hse.gov.uk/contact/faqs/manualhandling.htm (accessed 26 July 2012).
http://www.hse.gov.uk/news/subscribe/index.htm. (accessed 12 September 2012).
http://www.hse.gov.uk/myth/september.htm (accessed 25 July 2012).
http://www.hse.gov.uk/oshcr/index.htm (accessed 25 July 2012).
http://www.hse.gov.uk/pubns/books/l24.htm (accessed 26 July 2012).
http://www.hse.gov.uk/pubns/geis3.htm (accessed 8 October 2013).

http://www.hse.gov.uk/pubns/hse40.pdf (accessed 27 July 2012).
http://www.hse.gov.uk/pubns/indg174.pdf (accessed 26 July 2012).
http://www.hse.gov.uk/pubns/indg214.pdf (accessed 10 September 2012).
http://www.hse.gov.uk/pubns/indg223.pdf (accessed 26 July 2012).
http://www.hse.gov.uk/pubns/indg231.pdf (accessed 26 July 2012).
http://www.hse.gov.uk/pubns/indg232.pdf (accessed 31 July 2012).
http://www.hse.gov.uk/pubns/indg236.pdf (accessed 26 July 2012).
http://www.hse.gov.uk/pubns/indg244.pdf (accessed 26 July 2012).
http://www.hse.gov.uk/pubns/indg458.pdf (accessed 26 July 2012).
http://www.hse.gov.uk/pubns/indg291.pdf (accessed 27 July 2012).
http://www.hse.gov.uk/pubns/ais23.pdf (accessed 25 July 2012).
http://www.hse.gov.uk/riddor/report.htm (accessed 23 July 2012).
http://www.hse.gov.uk/risk/index.htm. (accessed 3 October 2013).
http://www.hse.gov.uk/risk/fivesteps.htm (accessed 26 July 2012).
http://www.hse.gov.uk/risk/theory/alarpglance.htm. (accessed 6 September 2012).
http://www.hse.gov.uk/toolbox/index.htm (accessed 11 September 2012).
http://www.hse.gov.uk/toolbox/workers/index.htm (accessed 3 October 2013).
http://www.hse.gov.uk/youngpeople/index.htm (accessed 6 September 2012).
http://www.hse.gov.uk/youngpeople/risks/ (accessed 3 October 2013).
http://www.hse.gov.uk/lau/publications/la-enforcement-code.htm?ebul=hsegen&cr=2/3-june-13.

Health Protection Agency (HPA)
http://www.hpa.org.uk/ (accessed 23 July 2012).

Home Office
http://www.isa.homeoffice.gov.uk/default.aspx?page=321 (accessed 23 July 2012).

Heuristic play
http://www.educationscotland.gov.uk/resources/h/genericresource_tcm4242264.asp (accessed 29 July 2012).

Literacy Trust
http://www.literacytrust.org.uk/early_years (accessed 30 July 2012).

National Day Nurseries Association (NDNA)
http://www.ndna.org.uk/ (accessed 22 October 2013).

NHS choice
http://www.nhs.uk/Livewell/Childrenssleep/Pages/babysleeptips.aspx (accessed 23 July 2012).

Ofsted
http://www.ofsted.gov.uk/resources/early-years-online-self-evaluation-form-sef-and-guidance-for-providers-delivering-early-years-founda. Ofsted (2013) 'Evaluation schedule for inspections of registered early years provision' (accessed 22 October 2013).
http://www.ofsted.gov.uk/resources/factsheet-childcare-registration-and-inspection-of-providers-who-hold-exemptions-learning-and-develo (accessed 25 July 2012).
http://www.ofsted.gov.uk/resources/compliance-investigation-and-enforcement-handbook (accessed 29 July 2012).
http://www.ofsted.gov.uk/resources/conducting-early-years-inspections.
Ofsted (2012) 'Conducting early years inspections' (accessed 4 September 2012).
http://www.ofsted.gov.uk/resources/are-you-ready-for-your-inspection-guide-inspections-of-provision-ofsteds-childcare-and-early-years-r.
Ofsted (2012) 'Are you ready for your inspection? A guide to inspections of provision on Ofsted's Childcare and Early Years Registers' (accessed 4 September 2012).
http://www.ofsted.gov.uk/resources/framework-for-regulation-of-provision-early-years-register.
Ofsted (2012) 'Framework for the regulation of provision on the Early Years Register'. (accessed 4 September 2012).

Ofsted Factsheet: 'Serious accidents, injuries and deaths that registered providers must notify to Ofsted and local child protection agencies'. http://www.ofsted.gov.uk/resources/factsheet-childcare-serious-accidents-injuries-and-deaths-registered-providers-must-notify-ofsted-an (accessed 29 July 2012).

Ofsted Factsheet: 'Giving medication to children in registered childcare'. http://www.ofsted.gov.uk/resources/factsheet-childcare-giving-medication-children-registered-childcare (accessed 27 September 2013)

Ofsted Factsheet: 'Childminders using assistants'. http://www.ofsted.gov.uk/resources/factsheet-childcare-childminders-using-assistants (accessed 29 July 2012).

Ofsted Factsheet: 'Requirements for written documents: childminders delivering the Early Years Foundation Stage (EYFS)'. http://www.ofsted.gov.uk/resources/factsheet-childcare-requirements-for-written-documents-childminders-delivering-early-years-foundation (accessed 29 July 2012).

Ofsted Factsheet: 'Requirements for the Childcare Register: childminders and home childcarers'. http://www.ofsted.gov.uk/resources/factsheet-childcare-requirements-for-childcare-register-childminders-and-home-childcarers (accessed 29 July 2012).

Ofsted Factsheet: 'Requirements for risk assessments'. http://www.ofsted.gov.uk/resources/factsheet-childcare-requirements-for-risk-assessments (accessed 29 July 2012).

Ofsted Factsheet: 'The requirements of the Early Years Register'. http://www.ofsted.gov.uk/resources/factsheet-childcare-requirements-of-early-years-register (accessed 29 July 2012).

Ofsted Factsheet: 'The numbers and ages of children that providers on the Early Years and Childcare Registers may care for'. http://www.ofsted.gov.uk/resources/factsheet-childcare-numbers-and-ages-of-children-providers-early-years-and-childcare-registers-may-c (accessed 29 July 2012).

Ofsted Factsheet: 'Requirements for the Childcare Register: childcare providers on non-domestic or domestic premises'. http://www.ofsted.gov.uk/resources/factsheet-childcare-requirements-for-childcare-register-childcare-providers-non-domestic-or-domestic (accessed 29 July 2012).

Ofsted Factsheet: 'Applying to waive disqualification'. http://www.ofsted.gov.uk/resources/applying-waive-disqualification (accessed 29 July 2012).

Ofsted Factsheet: 'Common core skills and knowledge'. http://www.ofsted.gov.uk/resources/factsheet-childcare-common-core-skills-and-knowledge (accessed 29 July 2012).

Ofsted Early Years Newsletters
http://www.ofsted.gov.uk/resources/early-years-june-2011 (accessed 29 July 2012).

Preschool Learning Alliance
https://www.pre-school.org.uk/ (accessed 22 October 2013).

Professional Association for Childcare and Early Years (PACEY)
http://www.pacey.org.uk/ (accessed 22 October 2013).

Royal Society for the Prevention of Accidents (ROSPA)
http://www.rospa.com/roadsafety/adviceandinformation/minibussafety/loading-safety.aspx (accessed 25 July 2012).
http://www.rospa.com/leisuresafety/playsafety/ (accessed 26 July 2012).

RHS; Potentially harmful garden plants
http://www.rhs.org.uk/Gardening/Sustainable-gardening/.../c_and_e_harmf... (accessed 30 July 2012).

Scottish Government
http://www.scotland.gov.uk (accessed 27 July 2012).

CookSafe (Scotland) http://www.food.gov.uk/scotland/safetyhygienescot/cooksafe/ (accessed 23 July 2012).

Serious case review; Daniel Pelka
Lock, R. (2013) Coventry Safeguarding Children Board. September 2013.
http://www.coventrylscb.org.uk/files/SCR/FINAL%20Overview%20Report%20%20DP%20130913%20Publication%20version.pdf (accessed 22 October 2013).

Serious case review; Keanu Williams
Lundberg, B. (2013) Birmingham Safeguarding Children Board. September 2013.
http://www.lscbbirmingham.org.uk/images/stories/downloads/executive-summaries/Case_25__Final_
Overview_Report_02.10.13.pdf (accessed 22 October 2013).

Serious case review; Little Stars Nursery Birmingham
Wonnacott, J. (2013) Birmingham Safeguarding Children Board. September 2013.
http://www.lscbbirmingham.org.uk/images/stories/downloads/executive-summaries/Published_Overview_
Report.pdf (accessed 22 October 2013).

Sun safety
http://www.sunsafenurseries.co.uk/ (accessed 30 July 2012).

Whistleblower advice
http://www.ofsted.gov.uk/contact-us/whistleblower-hotline (accessed 28 July 2012). http://www.pcaw.org.
uk/ (accessed 28 July 2012).

Appendix 1: Action plan

Action point	Action to be taken by (name)	Action to be completed by (date)	Date completed	Action checked by (name)

Action plan signed off by .... Date ....

Appendix 2:
Regulations summary for Early Years and BS EN standards on external and internal play equipment

Regulations summary for early years

The Early Years Foundation Stage (Welfare Requirements) Regulations 2007 [SI2007/1771]
www.legislation.gov.uk/uksi/2007/1771/contents/made

Early Years Foundation Stage (Welfare Requirements) Regulations 2012 [SI 2012/938]
www.legislation.gov.uk/uksi/2012/938/made

The Early Years Foundation Stage (Learning and Development Requirements) Order 2007 [SI2007/1772]
www.legislation.gov.uk/uksi/2007/1772/contents/made

Early Years Foundation Stage (Learning and Development Requirements) (Amendment) Order 2012
[SI2012/937] www.legislation.gov.uk/uksi/2012/937/contents/made

The Childcare (Early Years and General Childcare Registers) (Common Provisions) Regulations 2008
[SI2008/976] www.legislation.gov.uk/uksi/2008/976/contents/made

The Childcare (Early Years Register) Regulations 2008 [SI2008/974]
www.legislation.gov.uk/uksi/2008/974/contents/made

Childcare (Early Years Register) (Amendment) Regulations 2012 [SI2012/939]
www.legislation.gov.uk/uksi/2012/939/contents/made

The Childcare (General Childcare Register) Regulations 2008 [SI2008/975]
www.legislation.gov.uk/uksi/2008/975/contents/made

Childcare (General Childcare Register) (Amendment) Regulations 2012 [SI2012/1699]
www.legislation.gov.uk/uksi/2012/1699/contents/made

The Childcare (Inspections) Regulations 2008 [SI2008/1729]
www.legislation.gov.uk/uksi/2008/1729/contents/made

Childcare (Inspections) (Amendment and Revocation) Regulations 2012 [SI2012/1698]
www.legislation.gov.uk/uksi/2012/1698/made

The Childcare (Exemptions from Registration) Order 2008 [SI2008/979]
www.legislation.gov.uk/uksi/2008/979/contents/made

Childcare (Exemptions from Registration) (Amendment) Order 2010 [SI2010/744]
www.legislation.gov.uk/uksi/2010/744/contents/made

Childcare (Exemptions from Registration) (Amendment) Order 2011 [SI2011/584]
www.legislation.gov.uk/uksi/2011/584/made

The Early Years Foundation Stage (Exemptions from Learning and Development Requirements) Regulations
2008 [SI2008/1743] www.legislation.gov.uk/uksi/2008/1743/contents/made

The Childcare (Supply and Disclosure of Information) (England) Regulations 2007 [SI2007/722]
www.legislation.gov.uk/uksi/2007/722/contents/made

The Childcare (Supply and Disclosure of Information) (England) (Amendment) Regulations 2008 [SI2008/961] www.legislation.gov.uk/uksi/2008/961/contents/made

The Childcare (Fees) Regulations 2008 [SI2008/1804] www.legislation.gov.uk/uksi/2008/1804/contents/made

The Childcare (Fees) (Amendment) Regulations 2009 [2009 No. 1507] www.legislation.gov.uk/uksi/2009/1507/contents/made

Childcare (Fees) (Amendment) Regulations 2010 [SI2010/307] www.legislation.gov.uk/uksi/2010/307/contents/made

Childcare (Fees) (Amendment) Regulations 2011 [SI 2011/1628] www.legislation.gov.uk/uksi/2011/1628/regulation/2/made

The Childcare (Inspections) (Amendment) Regulations 2009 [2009 No. 1508] www.legislation.gov.uk/uksi/2009/1508/contents/made

The Childcare (General Childcare Register) (Amendment) Regulations 2009 [2009 No. 1545] www.legislation.gov.uk/uksi/2009/1545/contents/made

The Childcare (Disqualification) Regulations 2009 [2009 No. 1547] www.legislation.gov.uk/uksi/2009/1547/contents/made

Early Years Foundation Stage (Welfare Requirements) (Amendment) Regulations 2008 [SI 2008/1953] www.legislation.gov.uk/uksi/2008/1953/contents/made

The Early Years Foundation Stage (Welfare Requirements) (Amendment) Regulations 2009 [2009 No. 1549] www.legislation.gov.uk/uksi/2009/1549/contents/made

Source: Ofsted; 'Framework for the regulation of provision on the Early Years Register'. pp. 24–26 (May 2013); http://www.ofsted.gov.uk/resources/framework-for-regulation-of-provision-early-years-register (accessed 22 October 2013).

Summary of BS EN standards on external and internal play equipment

BS EN 1176-1:2008 Playground equipment and surfacing. General safety requirements and test methods

BS EN 1176-2:2008 Playground equipment and surfacing. Additional specific safety requirements and test methods for swings

BS EN 1176-3:2008 Playground equipment and surfacing. Additional specific safety requirements and test methods for slides

BS EN 1176-4:2008 Playground equipment and surfacing.

Additional specific safety requirements and test methods for cableways.

BS EN 1176-5:2008 Playground equipment and surfacing. Additional specific safety requirements and test methods for carousels

BS EN 1176-6:2008 Playground equipment and surfacing. Additional specific safety requirements and test methods for rocking equipment

BS EN 1176-7:2008 Playground equipment and surfacing. Guidance on installation, inspection, maintenance and operation

BS EN 1176-10:2008 Playground equipment and surfacing. Additional specific safety requirements and test methods for fully enclosed play equipment

BS EN 1176-11:2008 Playground equipment and surfacing. Additional specific safety requirements and test methods for spatial network

BS EN 1177:2008 Impact attenuating playground surfacing. Determination of critical fall height

BS 7188:1998+A2:2009 Impact absorbing playground surfacing. Performance requirements and test methods

BS 8409:2009 Fully enclosed play facilities. Code of practice

Whilst compliance with a British or European Standard is not a legal requirement, enforcement officers and courts view these standards as good practice. In an enforcement situation, or in the event of a civil claim for compensation for injury, a proprietor may have to provide objective evidence regarding the safety of their equipment, the installation and the effectiveness of their management procedures. Play equipment and how you manage play on equipment, for example through controlling age, numbers and supervision needs to be considered through risk assessment.